MORE

ANGUISHED
ENGLISH

MORE
ANGUISHED
ENGLISH

Richard Lederer

Illustrations by Bill Thompson

Delacorte  **Press**

Published by
Delacorte Press
Bantam Doubleday Dell Publishing Group, Inc.
1540 Broadway
New York, New York 10036

The trademark Delacorte Press® is registered in the U.S. Patent
and Trademark Office.

Library of Congress Cataloging in Publication Data

Lederer, Richard, 1938–
      More anguished English / Richard Lederer ; illustrations by Bill
   Thompson.
          p.   cm.
      ISBN 0-385-31017-X
      1. English language—Errors of usage—Humor.   I. Title.
   PN6231.E74L43   1993
   428'.00207—dc20   93-3000
                                                                 CIP

Manufactured in the United States of America

Published simultaneously in Canada

October 1993

10 9 8 7 6 5 4 3 2 1

BVG

to Simone

Contents

IV
The Tower of Babble

V
Thud and Blunder

Introduction

An unidentified job-seeker wrote on her application form, "I have an obsession for detail. I like to make sure I cross my i's and dot my t's."

A far-from-anonymous President George Bush shone blinding light on the self-evident when he proclaimed, "It's no exaggeration to say the undecideds could go one way or another."

A coed attending a college in northern Maine wrote in an essay, "I took up aerobics to help maintain my well-propositioned figure."

Across the nation, in Southern California, a man rushed into a law office to complain about a reporter who, he alleged, was slandering his good name. "I want to sue him for defecation of character!" the client exclaimed.

No slip is more showing than a slip of the pen or a slip of the tongue. And, perhaps, no slip provokes more hearty hilarity.

I have written *More Anguished English* simply because a half million readers of *Anguished English* have extracted from its pages the healthful effects of protracted laughter. "Laughter is an excellent workout for your body," states Dr. William Fry, a Stanford University psychiatrist and author. "A few seconds of hearty laughter match the benefits of a few minutes of vigorous exercise. A healthy guffaw stimulates air in the lungs, color in the cheeks, tone in the muscles, endorphins in the brain, and T-cells in the immune system. Protracted chuckling provides a workout for the face, shoulders, back, diaphragm, and abdomen, and massages right down to the toes and fingertips."

Laughter is also an elixir for the mind. Tests administered by Swedish psychologist Lars Ljungdahl before and after humor therapy reveal a reduction of stress and depression and a heightened sense of mental well-being and creativity. More and more, we are discovering that it only hurts when we *don't* laugh. Our five senses are incomplete without the sixth sense—our sense of humor.

My favorite testimonial about the benefits of imbibing the laughter arising from fluffs and flubs and goofs and gaffes came in a letter from Father Simon Sansome, of St. Joseph's Abbey in Spencer, Massachusetts: "I just finished reading *Anguished English*, my second reading. We monks are supposed to be silent and serious-minded so that many of my confreres are probably wondering about the muffled laughter issuing from my room. I can't read a page without violating our silence."

If laughter is the best medicine, Dr. Lederer recommends that you sip that medicine in this book slowly, as the following unsolicited statements make clear:

"Recently I was exposed to *Anguished English*. The doctor who repaired my split side says there should be no permanent damage from that problem, but he says he can't do anything about the residual involuntary smiling brought on by the illness."—*Doris Applebaum, Oak Park, Michigan*

"In this age of liability, I would strongly suggest

that you submit your manuscript to reputable health authorities for testing. It is my belief that the book need not be pulled from the shelves, but that a printed warning on the dust jacket will suffice. Perhaps the following could serve as a model:

" 'WARNING—The Surgeon General has determined that reading *Anguished English* could be hazardous to the health of persons with cardiopulmonary weakness. If you experience difficulty breathing or cardiac arrhythmia, cease reading immediately and think serious thoughts.' "—Yours for safer reading, *Edward M. Levin, Canaan, New Hampshire*

"I like to give your book to very special people on very special occasions. I must be careful about giving it to hospital patients after an operation. They tell me it tickles them so much it hurts their operation."—*Jerry Kannapel, Louisville, Kentucky*

"I was recently presented with a copy of *Anguished English*, and I am thinking of suing you for leaving me a crippled hysteric loaded with aches that threaten to be permanent. Promotion of any similar book should carry the caveat 'The Surgeon General warns that this book may be fatal unless read only in bed and aloud.' "—*Edward T. Barnard, Guilford, Connecticut*

The dictionary defines a gaffe as "a blunder; faux pas." *Faux pas* derives from the French word for "false step," and *gaffe* may descend from the French *gaff*, "a barbed spear used in landing large fish." Whether or not this etymology is accurate, many a super-duper blooper snooper has speared numerous humorous specimens, hauled them aboard, and shipped them to me. In this book, transfixed and wriggling, are the best of the catch. I thank the contributors, one and all, for their gifts of gaffes.

I express special gratitude to Dean William Hiss for most of the college admissions bloopers, to the

❧ I ❧
Classroom Classics

Rambo was a French poet.

Kids Write
the Darnedest Things

Take classrooms of students from elementary school through college, and mix thoroughly with smidgens of misinformation. Then shake up the concoction with examinations and essay assignments, and you have the perfect formula for student bloopers.

Fluffs and flubs miscreated by students illustrate Mark Twain's contention that the "most interesting information comes from children, for they tell all they know and then stop." While scribbling away in an exam room, students will often make history—that is, conjure up facts and events that have never existed:

- Early Egyptian women often wore a garment called a calasiris. It was a sheer dress which started beneath the breasts which hung to the floor.
- The great wall of China was built to keep out the mongrels.
- Pompeii was destroyed by an overflow of saliva from the Vatican.
- In 328 B.C. Rome was invaded by the Gals.
- Roman women built fires in their brassieres.

- Julius Caesar was renowned for his great strength. He threw a bridge across the Rhine. His dying words were "And you too—you brute!"
- Rome was invaded by the ballbearings.
- At the battle of Hastings the Angels and the Saxons were defeated by the Mormans.
- Joan of Arc was burnt to a steak.
- In the Middle Ages knights fought on horses. This was called jesting.
- Martin Luther was on a diet of worms.
- Henry VIII by his own efforts increased the population of England by 40,000.
- The title "Defender of the Faith" was given to Henry VIII after he was annulled.
- The death of Queen Elizabeth I ended an error.
- The two major religions of Ireland are Catholic and Prostitute.
- The pillory was where people were pubicly punished for their sins.
- John Paul Jones became one of America's great nasal heroes.
- The capital of Ethiopia is Adidas Ababa.
- In the middle of the eighteenth century all the morons moved to Utah.
- The difference between a president and a king is that a king has no vice.
- The system of checks and balances means that you have to keep a balance in the bank to write checks.
- Under President Adams there was the Alien and Sedation Act.
- The process of putting a president on trial is known as impalement.
- William Henry Harrison did not wear a coat and hat when he was sworn in as president and soon died of ammonia.

- Muckrakers were people who wrote about the sordid aspects of life such as Ida Tarbell.
- During his term of office, Woodrow Wilson had many foreign affairs.
- During the first twenty years of the century there was much suffrage from women.
- The leader of the Bolsheviks was John Lennon.
- In Hitler's Germany a huge anti-semantic movement arose.
- They are fighting a civil war in Serbia because the Bostonians, Crates, and Hertzgodivas want to get rid of the Serves.

A brand new English teacher in a small northern New Hampshire junior high school assigned her class the reading of *The Swiss Family Robinson*. This children's classic is about the adventures of a family marooned on a desert island. During the course of the story a large boa constrictor wraps itself around the family's donkey and devours the entire animal.

Here's how one of the seventh-graders described the incident: "The snake crept up, opened its jaws wide, and swallowed the ass whole."

Alas, in an age of cultural illiteracy, students aren't always very literary about literature:

- The two kinds of books printed are friction and non-friction.
- This is the best book I never read.
- Poetry is when every line starts with a capital letter and doesn't reach the right side of the page.
- My favorite myth was Jason and the Huguenots.
- Being between Scylla and Charybdis means that whichever way you go, you are going to get got.
- A fairy tale is something that never happened a long time ago.
- Chaucer was the father of English pottery.

- William Shakespeare was famous for writing and performing tragedies, comedies, and hysterectomies.
- The Montagues and the Capulets were fighting in the pubic square.
- Romeo and Juliet tell each other how much they are in love in the baloney scene.
- Romeo's last wish was to be laid by Juliet.
- In *The Merchant of Venice*, the Rialto is the business part of Venus.
- Brutus was a tragic hero in spite of dying in the end.
- During the banquet scene, Lady Macbeth was afraid that her husband would expose himself in front of the guests.
- Hamlet had an edible complex.
- Shakespeare wrote his plays in Islamic pentameter.
- Bacon was a man who thought he wrote Shakespeare.
- Rambo was a French poet.
- A great Jewish leader in Scotland was Rabbi Burns.
- Lord Byron wrote epics and swam the Hellespont. In between he made love drastically.
- The novels of Charles Dickens are mellow dramatic and full of truth and sediment.
- America's first president was Washington Irving.
- In *Drums Along the Mohawk*, while fleeing an Indian attack, the heroine hurriedly stuffed her enormous hams into a seat in the wagon.
- I like the story *The Last of the Moccasins*.
- Madame Bovary's problem was that she couldn't make love in the concrete.
- Harriet Beecher Stowe's famous novel about the evils of slavery was called *Uncle Tom's Cabinet*.

- In *The Scarlet Letter*, Hester Prynne and Arthur Dimmesdale had sexual intercoarse.
- And so, Hester Prynne had to stand up and show the scarlet letter to the community, which was clinging to her breast.
- Captain Ahab was abscessed by a White Whale in Herman Melville's *The Great White Dick*.
- In Ibsen's *Ghosts*, Oswald dies of congenial syphilis.
- In *Little Women*, Amy had an air of refinery about her.
- The Sherlock Holmes stories were written by Sir Arthur Cohen Doyle.
- Jake Barnes, in *The Sun Also Rises*, was injured in the groin region, and was impudent for the rest of his life.
- The theme of *The Catcher in the Rye* is that Holden Caulfield leaves the world of childhood and enters the world of adultery.

When it comes to music, students pull out all the stops and never just soft-pedal their ideas. In their compositions of the written kind, music students often play it by ear:

- Most authorities agree that music of antiquity was written a long time ago.
- An opera is a song of a bigly size.
- I know what a sestet is, but I'd rather not say.
- Music sung by two people at the same time is called a duel.
- A harp is a nude piano.
- Contralto is a low sort of music that only ladies sing.
- My favorite composer is opus.
- Agnus Dei was a woman composer famous for her church music.

- Stradivarius sold his violins on the open market with no strings attached.
- Even though he was deaf, Beethoven's symphonies were music to his ears.
- Do you know that if Beethoven were alive today, he'd be celebrating the 160th anniversary of his death?
- A very liked piece is the Bronze lullaby.
- Aaron Copland is one of our most famous contemporary composers. It is unusual to be contemporary. Most composers do not live until they are dead.
- In the last scene of *Pagliacci*, Canio stabs Nedda, who is the one he really loves. Pretty soon Silvio gets stabbed also, and they all live happily ever after.
- At one time, singers had to use musicians to accompany them. Since synthesizers came along, singers can now play with themselves.

Back in 1887, Mark Twain published a little essay called "English As She Is Taught," which presents "some quaint definitions of words," including:

Aborigines. A system of mountains.
Amenable. Any thing that is mean.
Equestrian. One who asks questions.
Franchise. Anything belonging to the French.
Parasite. A kind of umbrella.
Plagiarist. A writer of plays.

"It will be noticed," wrote Twain, "that in all these instances the sound of the word, or the look of it on paper, has misled the child." That tradition has continued unstinted. In all disciplines, students have brought the art of defining words to new heights—or should we say depths:

Absentee ballot. When you count the ballots and some of them aren't there.

Bigotry. Being married to two or more people.

Blasphemy. When you worship satin.

Celibacy. Something you put in a salad.

Crematorium. Where cream is made.

Darwinism. Survival of the fetus.

Foliage. A mother horse having a baby.

Husbandry. Having more than one husband.

Liberal. Free and generous, not bigtoed.

Marriage. A bond between two people to make their children literate.

Migration. A headache that birds get when they fly south for the winter.

Octopus. An eye doctor.

Phonetics. A class where we learn to have stress.

Prism. A place where they put criminals.

Syntax. Is all the money collected at church from sinners.

Tycoon. Something butterflies come out of.

Students of the world, rewrite! We who are about to grade salute you!

A molecule is so small that it can't be seen
by the naked observer.

Unscientific English

In their essays, quizzes, test papers, and lab reports, students have taught their teachers that Gutenberg was the inventor of removable type, William Tell discovered the telephone, and Thomas Edison invented the pornograph. Arkright invented a spinning machine, which he called a Spinny Jenny, after his wife. Later Samuel Crompton invented a similar machine, which he called a mule.

These inventive examples of science fiction and fantasy were concocted by junior high, high school, and college students around the world. It is truly astonishing what weird science our young (and not so young) Einsteins can create under the pressure of time and grades:

- Our new teacher told us all about fossils. Before she came to our class, I didn't know what a fossil looked like.
- Iron was first smelled in 1759.
- One horsepower is the amount of energy it takes to drag a horse 500 feet in one second.
- A squid is sort of like a small jellyfish, except that it has ten to twelve testicles that hang down from its body.

- Our biology class went out to explore the swamp and to collect little orgasms.
- The four stages of metamorphosis are egg, lava, pupil, adult.
- A super-saturated solution is one that holds more than it can hold.
- Americans throw away thousands of tons of food that some Asian child could be eating.
- The sun is a natural source of ultraviolent rays.
- We get our temperature three different ways. Either fairinheit, cellcius, or centipede.
- The sun makes one resolution every 24 hours.
- A city purifies its water supply by filtering the water and forcing it through an aviator.
- Part of the problem in trying to control population in the Third World is that it is against the people's religion to use preservatives.
- Sex is not only having two people going to bed to get rid of their frustration. It's what you get out of it. Sex can bring about trust and caring deeply for one another, which can create an endurable relationship.
- Isaac Newton passed the law of gravity.
- Pavlov studied the salvation of dogs.
- Franklin D. Roosevelt was crippled by Polyhole.
- My aunt won't be having any more kids because her tubes are tired.
- A molecule is so small that it can't be seen by the naked observer.
- Extinct birds lay very few eggs.
- A porcupine is an animal with many pricks.
- Without electricity we would still be in the dark ages.
- A liter is a nest of small animals.
- A magnet is something you will find in a bad apple.

- A permanent set of teeth consists of eight canines, two molars, and eight cuspidors.
- The pelvis protects the gentiles.
- In biology today, we digested a frog.
- Our heredity is determined by the number of jeans our mother and father gave us.
- To prevent head colds, use an agonizer to spray into your nose until it drops down into your throat.
- The big artery on your neck is called the jocular vein.
- The heart beats faster when you are younger, average when you are middle age, hardly at all when you are old, and not at all when you are dead.
- Between birth and seven years of age, the mother should be home with her children.
- Cider, the farmer's wine, is most refreshing. It tastes good with turkey, ham, and chicken. It is good with family, friends, and even strangers.
- I am pro-choice. Even to think that an unwanted pregnancy should last to full term is abdominable.
- Most of the people in the nation drink over 650 gallons of alcohol each year.
- A circle is a round straight line with a hole in the middle.
- To find the number of square feet in a room, you multiply the room by the number of feet.

Who knows? The Seattle student who wrote this description of human innards may be teaching in a college classroom by now:

The Body

The human body is composed of three parts: the Brainium, the Borax, and the Abominable Cavity.

The Brainium contains the brain. The Borax contains the lungs, the liver, and the living things. The Abominable Cavity contains the bowels, of which there are five: A, E, I, O, and U.

What may well be the all-time classic of classification is an essay written by a New Zealand pupil:

Birds and Beasts

The bird I am going to write about is the Owl. The owl cannot see at all in the day and is blind as a bat at night. I do not know much about the owl so I will go on to the Beast which I am going to choose. It is the Cow. The Cow is a mammal and it is tame. It has six sides: right, left, fore, back, upper, and below. At the back it has a tail in which is hanging a bush. With this it sends the flies away so they do not fall in the milk. The head is for the purpose of growing horns and so the mouth can be somewhere. They are to butt with. The mouth is to moo with.

Under the cow hangs the milk. It is arranged for milking. When the people milk the cow the milk comes and there is never any end to the supply. How the cow does it I have not learned but it makes more and more.

The man cow is called the ox. It is not a mammal. The cow does not eat much but what it eats it eats twice, so it gets enough. When it is hungry it moos and when it doesn't say anything it is because its insides is full of grass.

The cow has a fine sense of smell and you can smell it far away. That is the reason for the fresh air in the country.

In the Mist of Choosing Colleges

About five hundred years ago, the English poet Geoffrey Chaucer began publishing his epic *Canterbury Tales*, which he opened with these lines:

Whan that Aprill with his shoures soote
The droghte of March hath perced to the roote,
And bathed every vayne in swich licour
Of which vertue engendered is the flour.

In 1922, the poet T. S. Eliot looked at April through twentieth-century eyes and began his modern epic *The Waste Land* with the line "April is the cruelest month."

For many Americans April is indeed "the cruelest month" because it contains April 15, the deadline for filing income tax forms to the Internal Revenue Service. For many high-school students April 15 is an even more taxing day. On or around that date, thousands of high-school seniors receive letters informing them that they have or have not gained admission to the colleges of their parents' choice.

If the contents of the eagerly awaited envelope are thin, the news is probably bad. If the contents are thick with information about the college, the long

I have made the horror role every semester.

and arduous application process has probably been successful.

Caught up in the hurly-burly, helter-skelter, and hugger-mugger of college application, a student aspiring to enter Bates College once wrote, "I am in the mist of choosing colleges." William Hiss, the Dean of Admissions at Bates, has penetrated that mist by culling bloopers from the admissions essays that stream into the Lewiston, Maine, college. Most of the examples that follow are from Bill's ever-growing file:

- If there was a single word to describe me, that word would have to be "profectionist."
- I was abducted into the national honor society.
- So this is the essay that will get me into Bates. Let me tell you about mee.
- I function well as an individual and a group.
- In my senior year, I am serving as writting editor of the yearbook.
- I have made the horror role every semester.
- I want to be fully bilingual in three or more languages.
- I proliferate with English courses.
- I can read, speak, and write Greek fluently. My other two sports are tennis and volleyball.
- I would like to become a veterinarian. I have had some experience with animals. I have volunteered in dog kennels and cat houses.
- I like Bates because it is very private and small in stature.
- Bates is a college I can excell far in.
- Mathematics has hung like a stork around my neck.
- I am a freshman at Mount Holyoke College. I am considering going to Bates College for a year and

then possibly transferring. I applied as an undergraduate and was weight-listed.

- I have taken many curses in literature and writing.
- I am writing to tell you that I was very discouraged when I found out that I had been differed from Bates.
- At night we stayed in a youth hostile.
- I have a conscious which keeps everything in check.
- I have never been to New England, but from what I've heard it is a beautiful country.
- I want a small liberal in the northeast part of the country.
- Some things that make me different . . . is that I like to listen to a wide variety of music, for example Boston and Ratt.
- Bates is a small school that is not homogenized.
- So exists my idea of college. Perhaps I am chasing rainbows. But so I shall. I see now that one of them has B-A-T-E inscribed on it.
- Needles to say, . . .

Adulteration

A fifth-grade pupil wrote in an essay: "I have enjoyed my boyhood so much that I am looking forward to my adultery."

A young woman wrote to advice columnist Dorothy Dix, "I have been an adolescent for the past six or seven years. When will I grow up to be an adulteress?"

Eventually little boys and girls do grow up to become adults and adulteresses, at which point their clunky writing is supposed to get better. But that is not always the case. Many adults adulterate the language as much as students do. If you wonder why Johnny and Jane can't write, take a look at some of the work by their parents and teachers. We'll start with these poor excuses for excuse notes:

- Please excuse Raul from school yesterday. He had a stomach egg.
- Please excuse my daughter's absence. She had her periodicals.
- Susan was not at school yesterday because she had her first menopause.
- Stanley had to miss some school. He had an attack of whooping cranes in his chest.

From a basketball coach: "Mike has grown 6 feet in the last two years."

- Ralph was absent yesterday because of a sore trout.
- Please forgive Clarence for being absent from school the past few days. He was home sick from an operation. He had penis trouble and had to be serpent sized.
- Please excuse my daughter. She had abominable pain.
- I kept Monica at home today because she was not feeling too bright.
- Please excuse Jane Monday, Tuesday, and Wednesday. She had an absent tooth.
- Robert was late because he was not early. He is never in no hurry. He is too slow to be quick.
- The basement of our house got flooded where the children sleep so they had to be evaporated.
- Please excuse Connie from gym class to day, as she had difficulty breeding.

Would you recommend these teacher recommendations? Each was written in an apparent effort to help a student gain admission to a prep school or college:

- His news writing is accurate and inciteful to a degree highly unusual in someone his age.
- John is one of a rare bread.
- Jim infiltrated comfortably with the rest of the staff.
- Amy will be a definite addition to your class.
- Carol has all the abilities to compete at the top schools in the county.
- Dawn is seeking intellectual entanglement of the highest caliber.
- Her talent and strident practice routine has provided Peg with a variety of musical opportunities.

- *From a basketball coach:* Mike has grown 6 feet in the last two years.

Gaffes by teachers have caused many a class to come to a dead stop. The nuances of the frequently confused verbs *lie* and *lay* have created many a teacherly blush in classrooms throughout the land. At Northeastern University, in Boston, a journalism professor gave a usage test that included a question on the difference between the two troublesome verbs. As her students were handing in the test, she said, "I hope you all got *laid* right."

A Missouri English teacher once pointed out to her students that *lie* is an intransitive verb that means "repose" and can't take an object, while *lay* is a transitive verb that means "put" and always takes an object. "You can lay books on the desk, but you couldn't lay me on the desk," she continued.

"Wanna bet?" a student responded.

Embarrassing mistakes in the classroom are committed by pedagogues across the curriculum and at all levels of education. An English teacher at a Reno, Nevada, middle school announced to her class that the next book to be read would be Charles Dickens's *A Sale of Two Titties*. A Santa Monica, California, high school math teacher instructed his class to "find the circumcision of this circle." A Denver history teacher told the class to turn to the chapter on "World War Eleven."

A St. Joseph, Missouri, woman who worked as a guidance counselor said to a young man who had fallen asleep in her class, "Michael, if you don't wake up, you can just come into my office after school and sleep with me."

A Bonner Springs, Kansas, writing teacher told one of her students to direct his question to a boy sitting in the back of the room pecking away at a typewriter. "Why don't you ask that pecker?" she instructed.

In a famous New England boarding school during the 1960s, the teachers were called masters. In a faculty meeting, one of the masters complained loud and long about a troublesome student. After detailing the boy's shortcomings in his studies and general deportment, the teacher concluded, "He's got a very fresh mouth, and he criticizes his teachers both to their faces and behind their backs. He's the worst master baiter I've ever seen at this school!"

A Noxapater, Minnesota, teacher huffed at her class about a theft from her desk: "Someone has stooped so low as to take money out of my drawers!"

The members of a Winnipeg high school band were making too much noise as they warmed up for a concert. The bandmaster tried to quiet down the students with this admonition: "Class, while waiting to play your solo, please just finger your part; don't blow it."

An Aurora, Colorado, middle school teacher became annoyed by a student who kept playing with a Super Ball in class. After many warnings the teacher sent the boy to the office and wrote to the principal that "Johnny has been dismissed from my classroom because he will not stop playing with his balls in class."

As you might guess, there have been many variations on the tendency to ball up *ball* in a sentence. The best I've heard about was a public address announcement in a Missouri middle school: "Will the basketball team please report to the gym to have your photograph retaken. In the first picture your balls were cut off."

Somewhat on the same subject—a San Francisco high school teacher was known for giving difficult quizzes. Early one school year a female student asked him in class, "Are we going to be subjected to your tough little quizzies?"

"No," he replied sarcastically, "you're going to be seeing my tough big testies!"

One of the most learned of pedagogical improprieties escaped from the lips of a high school English teacher in Brooklyn. During a class discussion of the immigrant experience in America, he observed: "The traditional metaphor for our varied population used to be 'the melting pot.' But we have found that ethnic populations don't really melt in this country.

"A more accurate label is 'the ethnic stew.' Now class, think about a stew for a minute. In a stew, each ingredient contributes to the whole while retaining its discrete individuality. For example, in a stew the carrots retain their carrotness, the potatoes retain their potatoness—and the peas retain their peaness."

II

Misadventures in Blunderland

The Ladies Aid Society of the United Church will hold its annual potluck dinner Saturday in the church hall. Dinner will be gin at 5:30 P.M.

Parishable Goods

A Duluth, Minnesota, church maintained its own blood bank. Over the course of one particular year, a succession of needy parishioners had nearly drained the reserves. During the holiday season, the minister rose before the congregation and asked for help in the emergency: "I'm sure that with many of our college students back home for the holidays, there will be many extra pints around."

In a church bulletin, two articles appeared side by side. The first announced that the annual pageant would be the climax of the Lenten season. The second announced, "The Bishop is Coming!"

A large poster displayed outside London's St. Paul's Church proclaimed, "Christ Is Coming!" Right below it another sign read, "Please do not obstruct these gates."

On the gates of the Winnipeg Anglican cathedral, which is set in a cemetery, appear two notices: "The Anglican Church Welcomes You" and "The Premises are Protected by Guard Dogs."

Let the word go forth that some of the most light and enlightening bloopers are ones that appear in church and synagogue orders of services, bulletins, signs, newspaper reports, and sermons. I collect these blessed examples religiously because so many of them are simply divine:

- The Church is offering a series entitled "The Church Explores the Issues." Tomorrow's lecture will be "Recycling—Our Garbage is a Resource." There will be a potluck supper at 6 p.m.
- The outreach committee has enlisted 25 visitors to make calls on people who are not afflicted with any church.
- Miss Charlene Mason sang, "I Will Not Pass This Way Again," giving obvious pleasure to the congregation.
- *On a billboard in front of a church:*
  Morning Sermon: Jesus Walks on the Water
  Evening Sermon: Where is Jesus?
- Tonight's sermon: "What is Hell?" Come early and listen to our choir practice.
- God is Still On the Throne.
- The peace-making meeting scheduled for today has been canceled due to a conflict.
- Another ham and bean supper will be in the offering.
- Hymn: "Let All the World in Every Corner Sin."
- Last time we asked for prayer for Jerry Butler's foot. After nine months of various treatments, it's finally all gone.
- The Ladies Aid Society of the United Church will hold its annual potluck dinner Saturday in the church hall. Dinner will be gin at 5:30 p.m.
- The Rector would appreciate if the ladies of the parish would lend him their electric girdles for the pancake supper.
- During the service, Francis Bollinger, chorister, aroused the audience.
- The priest married John and Susan in the Rectum of the church.

- After an especially enthusiastic sermon, a parishioner told her Methodist minister: "Dr. Remington, I have to tell you that your sermon was so stirring that I went home and had a change of life."
- This week's youth discussion will be on teen suicide in the church basement.
- The poem "Our Church," by Vincent Gonzago, is one that each of us should immolate in our Christian witness.
- The wardens have decided to purchase a new coping machine for the church.
- *In the Travel section of a Minneapolis newspaper:* "Mexico celebrates Christmas with 'pastorellas,' pageants showing how the wise men and shepherds overcame obstacles and resisted temptations to visit Jesus at the manger."
- *In a Denver neighborhood newspaper:* On the day of his arrival, the pontiff is expected to celibate mass at Immaculate Conception Cathedral.
- *In a Louisville newspaper:* Reverend Hawley was congratulated on being able to get his parish plastered.
- *In a North Carolina newspaper:* His book, *They Walk with Angels,* is a copulation of hundreds of stories related to him by the church's evangelists.

A Connecticut newspaper reported that "more than 500 persons attended Friday night the final services of a two-week parish spiritual renewal at Our Lady of Mt. Carmel Church." Unfortunately, the headline to the article read, SPIRITUAL RENEWAL ENDS AT CHURCH. Other not-so-blessed headlines include:

ORGANIST TO GIVE ST. JOHN'S RECTAL

●

NUN TELLS HOW POPE TOUCHED HER:
SPREADS SEEDS OF ECUMENISM
THROUGHOUT SOUTH

●

VINELAND COUPLE TO TAKE ON
MISSIONARY POSITION

●

CROWDS RUSHING TO SEE POPE
TRAMPLE 6 TO DEATH

●

PIANIST TO PRESENT CONCERT OF SCARED
MUSIC THIS SUNDAY

●

BISHOP MCNULTEY DIES:
"HAD CLEAR VISION OF WHAT
THE CHURCH WANTED HIM TO DO"

The art teacher in a Maine elementary school also taught Sunday school, where she had the little ones draw pictures of Bible stories. Little Emma proudly presented her picture of the journey to Bethlehem. The drawing showed an airplane flying over the desert. In the passenger area were seated Joseph and Mary and little Jesus.

"The drawing is fine," said the teacher, "but who's that up front flying the plane?"

Answered Emma, "Why, that's Pontius the Pilot."

Sometimes the brightest pearls issue from the mouths of babes. When, during a service, the pastor intoned, "The peace of the Lord be with you," a three-year-old girl responded, "And pizza with you."

Here's a string of baubles from essays written in Sunday schools around the world:

- Noah's wife was called Joan of Ark.
- Lot's wife was a pillar of salt by day, but a ball of fire by night.
- Esau was a man who wrote fables and sold his copyright for a mess of potash.
- The brother of Jacob was called Seesaw.
- Samson pulled down the pillows of the temple.
- On Mount Sinai the Lord gave Moses the Ten Amendments.
- The Israelites made a golden calf because they didn't have enough gold to make a cow.
- The First Commandment was when Eve told Adam to eat the apple.
- The Fifth Commandment is humor thy father and mother.
- The Seventh Commandment is thou shalt not admit adultery.
- Joshua led the Hebrews in their victory in the battle of Geritol.
- Solomon had 200 wives and 700 cucumbers.
- Salome was a very wicked woman who wore very few clothes and took them off when she danced before Harrods.
- When Mary heard that she was the mother of Jesus, she sang the Magna Carta.
- Jesus was born because Mary had an immaculate contraption.
- When they arrived, they found Jesus in the manager.
- In the Gospel of Luke they named him Enamel.
- The people who followed the Lord were called the twelve opossums.
- The epistles were the wives of the apostles.
- Jesus ate the last supper with the twelve decibels.

- I love the Christmas story, especially the part about the three wise guys from the East Side.
- The Golden Rule says do one to others as they would do one to you.
- Another miracle is when Jesus rose from the dead and managed to get the tombstone off the entrance.
- A Christian can have only one wife. This is called monotony.
- The natives of Macedonia did not believe Paul, so he got stoned.
- The Pope lives in the vacuum.
- The Pope wrote a book called "The Pill's Grim Progress."
- The patron saint of travelers is St. Francis of Seasick.
- A republican is a sinner mentioned in the Bible.
- The Christians who were condemned to death entered the arena to face wild lions singing hymns of praise.
- The Romans went to the coliseum to watch the Christians die for the fun of it.
- A Protestant is a woman who gets her living through an immoral life.
- Holy acrimony is another name for marriage.

Court Jests

Hear ye! Hear ye!

Whereas the chapter titled "Disorder in the Court!" was judged to be one of the funniest in my book *Anguished English*, it is therefore fitting to present here and now a double docket of courtroom exchanges as they stand on record. Each example was taken down during actual court cases by certified court reporters and preserved for posterity.

Many people wonder what's wrong with the legal system. Well, one thing is that lawyers are trying cases and asking the strangest questions. You wouldn't believe some of the things that tumble out of lawyers' mouths in the heat of battle or the throes of boredom. Such situations can temporarily cause an attorney to lose brainpower, often with hilarious results. Let's sift through some of the evidence.

Exhibit A: Silly Questions. Remember, it takes years of law school and even more years of courtroom experience to be able to ask questions like these:

- You were there until the time you left, is that true?

Q. Could you see him from where you were standing?
A. I could see his head.
Q. And where was his head?
A. Just above the shoulders.

- So, besides your wife and children, do you have any other animals or pets?
- Now you have investigated other murders, have you not, where there has been a victim?
- Was that the same nose you broke as a child?
- In your opinion, how far apart were these vehicles at the exact time of collision?
- The 24th of December? Was that the day before Christmas?
- Were you alone or by yourself?
- Just how long have you known your brother?
- How many times have you committed suicide?
- Have you ever smelled an odorless solvent before?
- The question is simply designed to have you reflect for a moment and think if there is anything that stands out in your mind that in any way leads you to believe that you are not required to give an answer in whole to or in part to the pending question and all you are required to do is give me your firsthand impression of your firm belief right now as to whether any such fact or belief occurs to you as you sit here and think about it, as I am sure that you understand the question, but if you are the least bit confused, or if there is some word that there is some doubt about, I will have the reporter read the question and you can ask for clarification. Okay?

A reader of *Anguished English* forwarded me a cover letter sent to him by a Garden City, New York, law firm. The letter accompanied a draft of the reader's will: "Enclosed herewith please find draft copies of your Last Will and Testament. If the Will is acceptable, kindly advise our office so that we may schedule a convenient time for execution."

Is it no wonder, then, that our nation's court reporters have captured many a brain-dead query?

Q. I'll show you Exhibit 3 and ask if you recognize that picture.
A. That's me.
Q. Were you present when that picture was taken?

●

Q. Can you describe that individual?
A. He was about medium height and had a beard.
Q. Was this a male or a female?

●

Q. Have you ever tried to commit suicide?
A. Yes, sir.
Q. Were you ever successful?

●

Q. Answer the question. When did they have a knife at your throat?
A. That was a figure of speech.
Q. So they had a figure of speech at your throat?

●

Q. What is your relationship with the plaintiff?
A. She is my daughter.
Q. Was she your daughter on February 13, 1979?

●

Q. What did he do then?
A. He came home, and the next morning he was dead.

Q. So when he woke up the next morning, he was dead?

●

Q. Were you acquainted with the deceased?
A. Yes.
Q. Was this before or after she died?

●

Q. What happened then?
A. He told me, he says, "I have to kill you because you can identify me."
Q. Did he kill you?

●

Q. Is that a person you ever had any further dealings with after that?
A. He is dead.
Q. But did you have any further dealings with him after that?

●

Q. Do you remember everything that happened that night?
A. No, I don't remember it all.
Q. What part don't you remember about what happened that night?

●

Q. Was there some event, Martha, that occurred which kind of finally made you determine that you had to separate from your husband?
A. Yes.
Q. Did he try to do something to you?
A. Yes.
Q. What did he do?
A. Well, uh, he tried to kill me.

Q. All right. And then you felt that that was the last straw, is that correct?

•

Q. What were his motions?
A. To pull over out of the road.
Q. And he did that by giving you a hand signal and pointed his arm in the direction which he wanted you to go?
A. Yes.
Q. And he was alive when he was doing this?

I now offer Exhibit B: Acerbic Answers. When attorneys ask a Silly Question, they're spoiling for a Snappy Comeback:

Q. What is the meaning of sperm being present?
A. It indicates intercourse.
Q. Male sperm?
A. That is the only kind I know.

•

Q. Are you married, sir?
A. Yes.
Q. And to whom are you married?
A. My wife.

•

Q. Could you see him from where you were standing?
A. I could see his head.
Q. And where was his head?
A. Just above the shoulders.

•

MILITARY JUDGE. Any suggestions of what prevented this from being a murder trial instead of an attempted murder trial?
A. The victim lived.

●

Q. Were you leaning up against the shut door or open door?
A. A shut door. How can you lean against an open door? There's a hole there. You'd fall through the hole.

●

Q. Do you recall approximately the time that you examined the body of Mr. Dunnington at the Rose Chapel?
A. It was in the evening. The autopsy started about 8:30 p.m.
Q. And Mr. Dunnington was dead at that time, is that correct?
A. No, you dumb asshole, he was sitting there on the table wondering why I was doing an autopsy!

Q. Mr. Gonzales, can you read and write and understand the English language?
A. *Sí!*

Nothing but the Truth

ATTORNEY. Were you, too, shot in the fracas?
WITNESS. No, sir, I was shot midway between the fracas and the navel.

For decades, court reporters have collected bizarre courtroom exchanges. These records of disorder in the court they call "transquips." Capturing in shorthand every syllable uttered during hearings, depositions, trials, and sentencings, America's court reporters are literally America's keepers of the word.

H. L. Mencken once observed, "The penalty for laughing in a courtroom is six months; if it were not for this penalty, the jury would never hear the evidence." Transquips are the cracked side of the gripping trial scenes we see in movies and read about in novels. In real-life courtrooms, witnesses can say the darnedest things, and the high drama often turns into low comedy:

Q. Trooper, was the defendant obviously drunk when you arrested her?
DEFENSE COUNSEL. Objection, Your Honor. It calls for a conclusion.
JUDGE. Sustained.

Q. Trooper, when you stopped the defendant, were your red and blue lights flashing?

A. Yes, sir.

Q. Did the defendant say anything when she got out of her car?

A. Yes, sir.

Q. What did she say?

A. "What disco am I at?"

•

Q. You say this woman shot her husband with his pistol at close range.

A. Yes, sir, that's right.

Q. Any powder marks on his body?

A. Yes, sir, that's why she shot him.

•

Q. When was the first time you dropped out of class because of fatigue or memory problems?

A. I don't recall. I can't remember.

•

WITNESS. I started telling him, you know, look, I don't like the cussing and all the stuff.

Q. Does that irritate you, him swearing?

A. Yes, it does.

Q. What's he do next?

A. With both hands, drug me over to the bed, threw me around, and kept choking the shit out of me.

•

Q. When was the next occasion that you had difficulty with your wife?

A. April 27th, I believe it was, when she backed over me with the automobile.

●

Q. What is your date of birth?
A. October 1910.
Q. Do you remember the day?
A. No, but I've been told about it.

●

Q. Do you know whether your husband was born in wedlock?
A. No, he was born in Owen Sound.

●

Q. When was your last visit to Dr. Allenby?
A. I'll have to guess March or April.
Q. What was he doing to you?
A. He was trying to determine a reason that I couldn't maintain an erection.
Q. Do you have any plans to see him again?
A. Nothing firm, no.

●

Q. Are you seeing a psychiatrist now?
A. Yes.
Q. What's the psychiatrist's name?
A. Dr. Kwak.

●

Q. Do you have any stocks and bonds?
A. No.
Q. Do you have any debentures?
A. No, my teeth are my own.

●

JUDGE. Do you know what that oath you have just taken means?

DEFENDANT. Yeah. It means if I swear to lie, I gotta stick to it.

•

Q. You claim to have expertise in physics. Please tell us what Newton's first law is.
A. (Pause) Well, I don't believe I remember that.
Q. Who was Newton?
A. I believe he was the guy who came up with the first law.

•

Q. What are your duties here now?
A. We mainly check liquor violations, you could say minors in possession of alcoholic beverages, or check beer joints that they have all the city licenses and pay their taxes. Another function is that we do, we work on prostitutes.
Q. Is that something similar to the work you do in Narcotics?
A. Not necessarily. It's not—well, if you're asking for my opinion, it's not as dangerous.
Q. As far as the type of work, is it undercover, also?
A. In some cases you have to work undercover. If you are working on prostitutes, you go in an undercover role.

•

Q. You told her that before the surgery?
A. I said we could probably save the toes, but I don't know about the foot.

•

Q. Do you know the defendant?
A. Yes.

Q. Did you see the defendant shoot these people?
A. No. I seen it was Jimmy Jones.
Q. Do you know Jimmy Jones?
A. Yes, I know Jimmy Jones very well.
Q. And this man who you saw shoot these people, could you tell if he was white or black?
A. I don't know if he was white or black, but I know it was Jimmy Jones because I know Jimmy Jones.

●

Q. Mr. Gonzales, can you read and write and understand the English language?
A. *Sí.*

●

Q. So after anesthesia, when you came out of it, what did you observe with respect to your scalp?
A. I didn't see my scalp the whole time I was in the hospital.
Q. It was covered?
A. Yes, bandaged.
Q. Then, later on . . . what did you see?
A. I had skin graft. My whole buttocks and leg were removed and put on top of my head.

●

Q. You worked seven days a week?
A. A lot of times I worked more than that.

●

A. Uh-huh.
Q. You have to say "yes" or "no" so the court reporter can get it down. Is that a yes? You said, "Uh-huh."
A. Uh-huh.

•

Q. Where was the security officer in relation to you when you were struck by a car?
A. To my left.
Q. How far to your left?
A. I don't really remember. I was getting run over at the time.

•

Q. Do you perform any surgery, Doctor?
A. I do not perform surgery in the classical sense. Endoscopic procedures have been considered by third parties to be in the surgical class.
Q. Such as?
A. Such as gastroscopy, esophagoscopy, esophogastroduodenoscopy, and colonscopy, and endoscopic retrograde cholangiopancreatography.

•

Q. Did you notify Mr. Davis you wanted him to return the cab?
A. Yes, I sent him a letter to return the cab by registered mail.

•

COUNSEL. I have no further questions of this obviously incompetent witness.
THE WITNESS. Did you say "incontinent" or "incompetent"?
COUNSEL. Both. You are just pissing in the wind anyway.

•

COUNSEL. My objection is I would prophylactically object to any question.

JUDGE. Prophylactically?
COUNSEL. I am not talking about preventing contraception, Judge. I am talking about preventing the line of questioning that would be outside the scope of—
JUDGE. Your prophylactic objection is premature.
COUNSEL. I will withdraw it.

●

DEFENDANT. I can't pay the fine because I'm disabled.
JUDGE. What's your problem?
DEFENDANT. All my glands is prostrated.

This one has become a classic in the transquip field: Defendant, a fifteen-year-old boy accused of stealing a car and leading the police on a high-speed car chase, was appearing in juvenile court for the second time before the same judge.

DEFENDANT. But Judge, I did it for you.
JUDGE. What? You did it for me?
DEFENDANT. Oh, yes, Judge. That last time I was in trouble I promised you I would never get arrested again—and I was just trying to keep my promise.

●

Sometimes a jurist gets the chance to strike back with his or her gavel. A defendant pled, "Your Honor, as God is my judge, I didn't do it. I'm not guilty."
Replied the judge, "He isn't! I am! You did! You are!"

Outpatient: A person who has fainted.

Just for the Health of It

Doctors are generally very smart people. I know because, over the years, some of the most articulate and knowledgeable letters about language that I have received are from members of the medical profession.

But doctors sometimes find it as hard as anyone else to say what they mean. Like everyone else, doctors can occasionally be tongue-depressing, even when they are describing cases. Physicians, heal thyselves!

The tradition of medical mutilation of the English language goes back hundreds of years. Research into early nineteenth-century Missouri death records has produced some curious medical reports; among the causes of death listed were:

- Went to bed feeling well, but woke up dead.
- Died suddenly, nothing serious.
- Cause of death unknown; had never been fatally ill before.
- Don't know; died without the aid of a physician.
- Death caused by blow on the head with an ax. Contributory cause, another man's wife.

Here is an off-the-charts lineup of more recent medical fluffs and flubs as actually dictated by doctors around the world. To my knowledge, each nugget in this varicose vein of anguished English has in no way been doctored. Fortunately for the rest of us, unless we happen to be one of the patients, these classics in the annals of curative history have been saved for posterity by medical transcriptionists, who apparently love to have a little fun while taking their jobs seriously:

- The left leg became numb at times and she walked it off.
- By the time he was admitted, his rapid heart had stopped, and he was feeling better.
- Patient has chest pain if she lies on her left side for over a year.
- Prior to patient's birth, she was informed at all times that her pregnancy was a normal one.
- The patient states there is a burning pain in his penis which goes to his feet.
- Both the patient and the nurse herself reported passing flatus.
- His daughter was given a genealogical examination at the hospital.
- On the second day the knee was better and on the third day it had completely disappeared.
- She has had no rigors or shaking chills, but her husband states she was very hot in bed last night.
- This patient has been under many psychiatrists in the past.
- The patient has been depressed ever since she began seeing me in 1983.
- The pelvic examination will be done later on the floor.
- The patient has never been pregnant and denies any reason for this.

- She was divorced last April. No other serious illness.
- The patient was admitted with abdominal pain from the emergency room.
- He was found lying on the bathroom floor by his wife.
- Patient was seen in consultation by Dr. Blank, who felt we should sit tight on the abdomen and I agreed.
- Patient stated that if she would lie down, within 2–3 minutes something would come across her abdomen and knock her up.
- Preoperative diagnosis: herniated dick.
- I will be happy to go into her GI system; she seems ready and anxious.
- Patient was released to outpatient department without dressing.
- I have suggested that he loosen his pants before standing, and then, when he stands with the help of his wife, they should fall to the floor.
- The patient is a three-year-old who has been vomiting off and on for twelve years.
- Patient had bilateral varicosities below her legs.
- The patient is tearful and crying constantly. She also appears to be depressed.
- Dr. Blank is watching his prostate.
- Sister Anna Maria is a Catholic nun who is currently in between missionaries.
- The patient was advised not to go around exposing himself to other people.
- Rectal exam is deferred because patient is sitting upright.
- The patient was somewhat agitated and had to be encouraged to feed and eat himself.
- Discharge status: Alive but without permission.

- The patient will need disposition, and therefore we will get Dr. Blank to dispose of him.
- The patient does not smoke or drink alcohol.
- Coming from Detroit, Michigan, this man has no children.
- Patient was admitted and suffered severe pain by Dr. Blank.
- Healthy appearing decrepit 69-year-old white female, mentally alert but forgetful.
- When you pin him down, he has some slowing of the stream.
- Dr. Blank will dictate on the right breast later.
- The infant was handed to the pediatrician, who cried spontaneously.
- The patient was found to have twelve children by Dr. Blank.
- She was treated with Mycostatin oral suppositories.
- Many years ago the patient had frostbite of the right shoe.
- The patient is a 74-year-old white female who was brought to the ER by paramedics acutely short of breath.
- After his release from Coronary Care, Dr. Blank worked him over.
- Pain in his ear with inability to breathe through his ear.
- The patient developed a puffy right eye, which was felt to be caused by an insect bite by an ophthalmologist.
- The patient refused an autopsy.
- The patient has no past history of suicides.
- The patient expired on the floor uneventfully.
- Patient left his white blood cells at another hospital.
- Apparently the mother resented the fact that she was born in her forties.

- Patient was becoming more demented with urinary frequency.
- Physician has been following the patient's breast for six years.
- This unfortunate 45-year-old woman has known me for about eight years.
- The patient is a 79-year-old widow who no longer lives with her husband.
- The patient's past medical history has been remarkably insignificant with only a 40-pound weight gain in the past three days.
- The right front side of her car was broadsided while the patient was in the passenger seat going through the intersection.
- The patient is a smoker so will be admitted to a smoking bed.
- The nursing home where the patient lives was noted to sputter, cough, and run a fever.
- The bugs that grew out of her urine were cultured in the ER and are not available. I WILL FIND THEM!!!
- He had a left-toe amputation one month ago. He also had a left above-knee amputation last year.
- The patient is a 71-year-old female who fractured her little finger while beating up a cake.
- She slipped on the ice and apparently her legs went in separate directions in early December.
- The patient has a high IQ and belongs to Mensis.
- The patient left the hospital feeling much better except for her original complaints.
- The operative field appeared in good condition, with no bleeding, and therefore the patient was terminated.
- The patient experienced sudden onset of severe shortness of breath with a picture of acute pulmonary edema at home while having sex which gradually deteriorated in the emergency room.

Bless the medical transcriptionists who have preserved these boners and boo-boos as a benefit to the health of all of us. May their tribe thrive and multiply!

For more medical madness, have a look at *A Bloopered Guide to Medical Terminology:*

Abdominal. Terrible.
Anatomy. Part of a moleculey.
Appendix. End of a book.
Artery. The study of fine paintings.
Atrophy. A prize.
Bacteria. Inconveniently located room for serving food.
Barium. What you do when CPR fails.
Benign. What you do after you be eight.
Bowel. A letter like *a, e, i, o,* or *u.*
Capillary. What comes before a butterfly.
Cardiac. An automobile nut.
Cataract. An expensive imported car in Japan.
CAT scan. Searching for kitty.
Cauterize. Made eye contact with her.
Cesarean section. A district in Rome.
Chiropractor. Egyptian doctor.
Colic. A sheepdog.
Coma. A punctuation mark.
Congenital. Friendly.
Dilate. To live too long.
Enema. Opposite of a friend (literally!).
Esophagus. Egyptian burial casket.
Fester. Quicker.
Fibula. A small lie.
Gangrene. Worn on St. Patrick's Day.
Genital. Non-Jewish.
G. I. series. Baseball games between teams of soldiers.

Goiter. Stocking holder.
Grippe. A suitcase.
Hangnail. A coat hook.
Hemoglobin. Half the world.
Impotent. Distinguished, well known.
Intestine. Without a will.
Kidney. Young person's leg joint.
Lumbar. Wood.
Mammography. Biography about a southern mother.
Medical staff. A doctor's cane.
Microbe. What you wear when you are speaking in front of a large audience.
Minor operation. Coal digging.
Morbid. A higher offer.
Neurosis. Budding flowers.
Nitrate. Lower than the day rate.
Node. Was aware of.
Organic. Church musician.
Outpatient. A person who has fainted.
Pedicure. Bicycle repair.
Postoperative. A letter carrier.
Prostate. For government.
Protein. In favor of young people.
Pulmonary. Referring to railroad cars.
Recovery room. Place to do upholstery.
Secretion. Hiding something.
Seizure. Roman emperor.
Serology. Study of English knighthood.
Serum. Burn 'em.
Specimen. Jewish astronaut.
Splint. A quick run in Tokyo.
Spine. A country next to France.
Surgeon. A fish.
Tablet. A small table.
Terminal illness. Getting sick while waiting for the bus.

Tourniquet. Tennis competition.

Tumor. An extra pair.

Urine. Opposite of "You're out."

Varicose veins. Veins that are close together.

Vertigo. What a tour guidebook tells you.

Vitamin. What to do with guests who come to your house.

X ray. A suggestive ray, X-rated.

Zinc. Where you wash your face.

Sign Language

In the October 3, 1988, issue of *People* magazine appeared a two-page feature on *Anguished English* and a profile of my life as a fly-by-the-roof-of-the-mouth, user-friendly linguist and wizard of idiom.

After William Sonzski, the writer of the piece, came up to my home to interview me, the next month, his partner, Richard Howard, arrived for a two-day photography session. Richard telephoned me a week before his visit and asked me to think about setting up a humorous, posed picture that would somehow summarize my work and lead into the article.

"How can linguistic activity be captured in a photograph?" I asked myself.

"In a sign," came the answer.

But what sign was conveniently nearby, obviously funny to all readers, and not embarrassing to a particular business or individual?

The solution immediately presented itself. On the outskirts of my town stands a telephone pole with the street sign ELECTRIC AVENUE. And, sure enough, right below it is a yellow diamond traffic sign announcing NO OUTLET.

On a raw April afternoon, I mounted a stepladder

and, with Richard Howard's camera snapping away, I ogled and grimaced at ELECTRIC AVENUE/NO OUTLET for an hour and a half. One of these photographs did indeed become the lead-in for the *People* feature.

Our nation is festooned with signs of life, signs that may confuse more than they inform:

Two signs on a pole in Newburyport, Massachusetts: COFFIN LANE/DEAD END.

Street sign next to a Salem, Massachusetts, cemetery: ONE WAY/EXIT ONLY.

In the entrance of a Manhattan camera store:
NO
DOGS
EATING
BICYCLES

In the window of an Atlanta clothing store: Sid's Pants is Open.

On a California freeway: Fine For Littering.

On the wall of a British Columbia cleaning service: Able to Do the Worst Possible Job.

In each room in a London hotel: If you wish for breakfast, lift the telephone and ask for room service. This will be enough to bring your food up.

In a Memphis barber shop: Hair cut while you wait.

In a Bedford, New Hampshire, restaurant: Free dinner on your birthday. If today is your birthday, show us a valid driver's license as proof, and you will get your entree free. One a year only.

In a New York jewelry store: Genuine Faux Pearls.

In a Kansas City oculist's office: Broken lenses duplicated here.

At the Concord, New Hampshire, landfill: All Cars Must Stop Here and Come to Window.

On the door of a Manhattan establishment: This door is alarmed 24 hours a day.

In a Boston fast-food parking lot: Parking for Drive-Through Customers Only.

In an Auburn, Maine, restaurant: We fry cholesterol free.

Nailed to trees all along rural roads around Shreveport, Louisiana: Frank's Body Works.

Billboard on Florida highway: If You Can't Read, We Can Help.

On the Triborough Bridge in New York: In Event of Air Attack Drive Off Bridge.

Posted at a Santa Fe, New Mexico, gas station: We refuse to sell gas to anyone in a glass container.

In a Dallas company outlet store: One case per customer regardless of size.

Conspicuously displayed in many restaurants: Please wait for hostess to be seated.

In front of an upstate New York house: Yard Sale Inside House.

Displayed by an Atlanta street vendor: Fresh Flowers/Get Some Tonight.

In Laconia, New Hampshire: Executive Diaper Service.

On a diner standing near a Pittsburgh bus station: Terminal Lunch.

In the ladies' room of a Mass Pike rest stop: Employees must wash hands before handling food with soap and water and dry thoroughly.

On a Lockhart, Texas, gas station and minimart: We're out of Rolaids, but we've got gas.

In an Atlanta Laundromat: Do not overpack the washers. It causes overloading.

In a Des Moines Laundromat: Anyone caught tampering with the machines will be persecuted.

*At the basketball court in a Gastonton, North Caro-

lina, YMCA: Anyone caught hanging from the rim will be suspended.

In a New Hampshire supermarket: Photo Customers: For one-day service, film must be dropped off prior to 12:00 noon the previous day.

Posted in a Canadian hospital: Flu doesn't take a holiday and neither do we!—Memorial Hospital/Closed Thanksgiving Day.

On a Rapid City store: Give That Bride a Good Case of Worms or Other Fine Bait.

On a Portland, Maine, building: Depressed storm drains.

In a Sioux City parking lot: No Parking at anytime —Violators will be impounded.

On the door of an Ellsworth, Maine, restaurant: The Indian Trading Post will be closed for Yom Kippur.

On the entrance of a Burlington, Ontario, parking lot: Any car parked on this property will be towed away at owners expense and will be prosecuted.

On a trash can in a Meriden, New Hampshire, school (presumably meant for the janitors): Empty when full.

Left behind by an Atlanta company: HELLO, your home has just been exterminated by Ray Russell and Company.

On the gate of a Concord, New Hampshire, high school:

EMERGENCY EXIT
DO NOT BLOCK
NO VEHICLES BEYOND THIS POINT

In a Grand Rapids restaurant: Half baked chicken.

In a Dayton barbershop: During vacation of owner, a competent hair stylist will be here.

In a San Marcos, Texas, furniture store: All credit approvals must have approved credit.

On a Healdsburg, California, bed-and-breakfast: Please excuse our improvements.

On a Jacksonville, Florida, bookstore: Rare, out-of-print, and nonexistent books.

At London's Heathrow Airport: No Exit for Passengers.

On a construction office in England: We Specialize In Quick Erections.

On a library in Marlboro, New Hampshire, honoring Robert Frost: Frost Free Library.

On many a garment bag: To avoid suffocation, keep away from children.

III

Stop the Presses!

An antique mirror was stolen from the home of Mr. and
Mrs. Buddy Shavers of Worcester Thursday evening. Police
are looking into it.

Rot off the Press

Americans are great newspaper readers. Four of five adults read the newspaper regularly, and nearly 90 percent of American homes have newspapers in them. This vast readership of 110 million keeps about ten thousand weeklies and seventeen hundred daily papers in business.

News stories have short lives. A story is born when something happens and dies when the newspaper gets old—usually in less than a day. Sometimes, though, under the press of constant press deadlines, a reporter or editor will goof, and part of a story will live on beyond its time—in a collection of anguished English:

- Bush, himself a former director of the CIA, said Gates would not routinely attend Cabinet meetings but would take part in sessions where intelligence was necessary for making decisions.
- Elias and other researchers say they believe that aspartame can do more damage over a long period of time than federal health officials.
- More women tend to fall victim when strong earthquakes hit because they look after the aged and children, while men tend to evacuate imme-

diately, the Tokyo Metropolitan University reported Monday.

- The Women's Club met Tuesday at the home of Mrs. Layton. Mrs. Knight gave a review of the book *Naked Came I*, after which Mrs. Farwell gave a demonstration.

- This is the time of year when all the policemen and firemen hold their balls.

- By then, she will have shed 80 of the 240 pounds she weighed in with when she entered the Peter Bent Brigham hospital obesity program. A third of her left behind!

- Inflation and spending cuts have forced the rewriting of a fairy tale. Because of cash restrictions imposed by Wolverhampton Council, the Open Air Theatre Company has lost some of its members and will stage "Snow White and the Two Dwarfs."

- THANKS to two special people who picked my wife up after a fall from her bike and broke her pelvis and severely damaged her back and many other parts of her body. Jim and Betty Kelleher—there are not enough words to express my gratitude and heartfelt thanks for you and what you did for my wonderful wife.

- We want to wish all our Jewish friends a happy Yom Kippur.

- He then gave up cricket for a missionary position in Rhodesia.

- The pH of our well is 5.6. Is this acidic enough to worry about? We also have a problem with darkening toilet bowls, but the water tastes great.

- The 37-year-old daughter of Queen Elizabeth II and her horse finished fourth in the national Hunt Race at Hereford.

- One thousand marijuana plants have been seized in a joint police investigation near here Monday.

- They have suspended hangings in South Africa now.
- An antique mirror was stolen from the home of Mr. and Mrs. Buddy Shavers of Worcester Thursday evening. Police are looking into it.
- Dr. Krieger is married. His wife, Vanessa, is a Special Education.
- This evening's meeting of the Clairvoyance Society has been canceled due to unforeseen circumstances.
- This evening's entertainment is provided free of charge to all individuals with developmental disabilities, their parents or guardians.
- Brian Porter, embezzler, endorsed checks for $90,299.77 last year. For nine months he played the daily double, sipped dry martinis, dallied with expensive prostitutes, flew first class city to city, and spent the rest foolishly.
- Perski explained to reporters the reason the police blotter is no longer easily accessible to the public is because private security agencies, insurance people, lawyers, and other criminals were looking at it for their own personal benefit.
- The first was the deputy secretary of state, regarded by the White House inner circle as a man of loyalty and capability, qualities whose importance to a White House cannot be underestimated.
- Other planned features of the store: . . . About 100 more employees, on top of the 125 to 150 new sales consultants hired in August.
- Mayor Gary P. Ryan said Pepper Pike will begin next week working with county health officials to try to convince the birds to move, perhaps by setting off firecrackers and other noisemakers to get the flocks out of there.
- The macadamia was named for Dr. John Mac-

Adam, an enthusiastic scientist who promoted the nut in its native Australia, and was dubbed "the perfect nut" by Luther Burbank.

- A high-ticket dinner at the exclusive Fox Run Golf Club drew about 50 supporters, including Mel Scarborough, who at one time lived in Bensonville and also harbored some exotic animals, and his wife, Lorraine.

- President Nixon today proclaimed May "Older Americans Month." In a second proclamation, Nixon also designated May as "National Arthritis Month."

- According to officials, it took the clever plan of assistant chief Robert Clark to free the men. Clark hooked up a wench to a pickup truck, then hoisted the men to freedom.

- CARD OF THANKS. On behalf of Barbara Rutledge and her family, our sincere thanks go out to those sending flowers, cards and contributing to the death of her husband.

- Twelve shoppers on a crowded Brooklyn thoroughfare were injured yesterday, when a 65-year-old woman lost control of her car, mounted the curb, and ran for 40 feet among pedestrians on the sidewalk.

- The candidate looked younger than his 39 years, full of energy, and his sandy hair, stylishly cut and blow-dried, danced as he moved his 6 feet around the stage.

- Dear Sir: I am a married woman, and I am fed up with being stuck at home. I wondered if you could help me as I am thinking of starting to breed with my poodle.

- Police Officer Avery Williamson relied on intuitive judgment when he exposed himself to an armed suspect who had abducted two children. The gamble paid off when the man surrendered.

- The airplane was attempting a loop and was only a few feet from the ground when it crashed, witnesses said.
- With the exception of victimless crimes (which need not concern us here), every single crime committed in this nation of ours involves a victim.
- A purple lady's bicycle was missing from Serendipity Lane recently.
- A delay in deciding whether state employees would be made monthly, twice a month, or every two weeks was criticized today.
- Ms. Pinkus graduated from Rensselaer Polytechnic Institute in New York with a degree in bachelor's architecture.
- Chairman Billings asked Board members to muster support from parent-teacher groups to support the governor's task force on drinking while intoxicated.
- Dr. Capper has done more than 1,200 open-ended vasectomies.
- State police charged Judson with firing several gunshots into a Montgomery Township mobile home occupied by four persons and a pickup truck last November.
- The three-day outing is climaxed by a huge picnic, which practically doubles the town population each year.
- The bride was wearing a gorgeous old lace gown that fell to the floor as she came down the aisle.
- He hasn't even had his day in court yet, but Simon Wynne has been kicked off the ESU basketball team after being arrested and accused of driving a parked car while intoxicated.
- A bird walk will take place at White Memorial Conservation Center on Saturday, at 2 p.m., at the nature museum entrance. Leader Steve

Fischer of Baldwin has led bird walks lasting up to several days as far away as Costa Rica.

- Responding to complaints that persons had been seen urinating in the yard, Ordway offered to install an 8-foot-high cedar fence.
- Montreal police don't hesitate to use whatever laws, regulations, or persuasion they feel they need to control morality in the city and prevent it from getting a foothold in any one part of the city.
- A college friendship that began a year ago ended in matrimony yesterday.
- The visibly shaken woman, wearing handcuffs and leg irons, fell halfway up the stairs on her way to the courtroom.
- For 35 years I have fished Long Pond and have taken out visitors from all over the United States.
- The ladies bathroom is manned at all times.
- The plane apparently flew directly into the hillside and was heavily demolished.
- We note with regret that Mr. Vincent Avallone is recovering after a serious accident.
- A son was born to Mr. and Mrs. Charles Mulkahey, Garrison St., during the past week. Congratulations, Pete!
- Jim Ray Jolliet, Ihnman's attorney, put his hands over his eyes when the verdict was announced. He rested the other hand on Ihnman's shoulder.
- Sheriff Nance said the leopard had been spotted. . . .
- *In a review of Shakespeare's* A Midsummer Night's Dream: The best I have ever seen, with David Waller's virile Bottom particularly splendid.
- Smith smashed a towering shot that hit a popcorn vendor on the fly.
- I would like to thank everyone for their cards and

contributions in memory of my beloved husband, father, and grandfather.

- "Sievers will be a great insurance policy for us," said the White Sox manager, Al Lopez. "He can spell Ted Kluszewski at first base."

- Irving Rothstein is a Washington writer who specializes in manufacturing issues.

- Two of Indiana's five former living governors don't think much of the state's lottery.

- Colorado's wildlife officers are investigating the second death of a bull moose.

- We have made the commitment to our readers to minimize "jumps," those stories that continue from one page to another. Readers have told newspapers loud and often that they do not like such "jumps," and most stories will fit on the page they begin.—See CHANGE, page A-2.

- Osborne chased it around the back of the net, dug the puck off the boards, and fired a pass to Poddubny, who beat Buffalo goaltender Tom Barrasso between the legs.

- *Letter to advice columnist Dorothy Dix:* My husband keeps telling me to go to Hell. Have I a legal right to take the children?

- *Heard on a New Hampshire radio station:* A group of pornographic publishers has been arrested in Fellows Balls, Vermont.

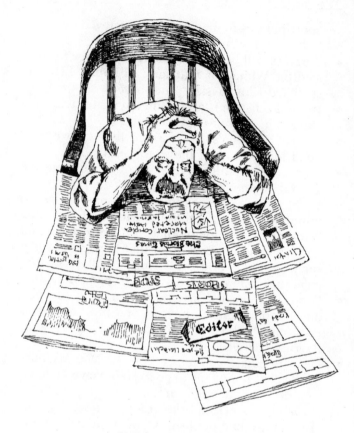

Two-headed headlines
blither double meanings.

The English language and the game of baseball would be immeasurably poorer without the fractured diction and unruly grammar of St. Louis pitcher and broadcaster Dizzy Dean. Dizzy peppered his commentary with *ain't*s and double negatives, and when he thought a verb too colorless, he invented his own, such as "He slud into third base" or "The pitcher flang the ball." When an indignant listener complained, "Mr. Dean, don't you know the King's English?" Dizzy reflected for a moment, then replied, "Sure I do—and so's the Queen."

During the 1934 World Series, Dean tried to break up a double play and was struck in the head by the relay throw. The force of the ball knocked him unconscious and sent the daffy pitcher to the hospital.

Luckily Dean was not seriously injured. The next day, a headline read X RAYS OF DEAN'S HEAD REVEAL NOTHING.

That Dizzy headline is a nonpareil among pareils when it comes to two-headed headlines that blither double meanings. Here are some other bold-faced double entendres that leave editors and publishers crimson-cheeked:

MAN STRUCK BY LIGHTNING
FACES BATTERY CHARGE

•

NEW STUDY OF OBESITY
LOOKS FOR LARGER TEST GROUP

•

ASTRONAUT TAKES BLAME
FOR GAS IN SPACECRAFT

•

KIDS MAKE NUTRITIOUS SNACKS

•

5½ FOOT BOA CAUGHT IN TOILET;
WOMAN RELIEVED

•

CHEF THROWS HIS HEART
INTO HELPING FEED NEEDY

•

AIRLINER IS HELD UP FOR 3 HOURS
BY MAN ARMED WITH AX

•

ARSON SUSPECT IS HELD
IN MASSACHUSETTS FIRE

•

BRITISH UNION FINDS DWARFS
IN SHORT SUPPLY

•

LAWMAKERS BACK TRAIN THROUGH IOWA

●

CAROLINA INN LOSES LICENSE FOR RACISM

●

BAN ON SOLICITING DEAD IN TROTWOOD

●

CAUSE OF ODOR IN BARNSTEAD
HAS BEEN FOUND: CRENSHAW

●

LANSING RESIDENTS CAN DROP OFF TREES

●

KIDNEY PATIENTS TO GO ON THEIR OWN

●

LOCAL HIGH SCHOOL DROPOUTS
CUT IN HALF

●

FOOD PROCESSORS TURN TO PLASTIC

●

NEW VACCINE MAY CONTAIN RABIES

●

MAN MINUS EAR WAIVES HEARING

●

DEAF COLLEGE OPENS DOORS TO HEARING

●

AIR HEAD FIRED

●

STEALS CLOCK, FACES TIME

•

BE SURE TO EAT RIGHT BEFORE SURGERY

•

PROSECUTOR RELEASES PROBE
INTO UNDERSHERIFF

•

DISMEMBERMENT KILLER CONVICTED:
THANK GOD JURY COULD
PUT PIECES TOGETHER

•

HERE'S HOW YOU CAN LICK
DOBERMAN'S LEG SORES

•

CERVICAL CANCER LINKED
TO SMOKING IN A STUDY

•

INTERNAL MEMOS
ON TAMPON INTRODUCED

•

OLD SCHOOL PILLARS
ARE REPLACED BY ALUMNI

•

BANK DRIVE-IN WINDOW
BLOCKED BY BOARD

•

ROCK STAR HOT WITH SICK CHILD

airport? When a headline blares POLICE ACT TO STOP URINATING IN PUBLIC, we wonder who exactly are the ones relieving themselves and we laugh at the comic relief that such a headline provides:

MARRIAGE LICENSE PERMITS MOUNTING

•

WHY YOU WANT SEX CHANGES WITH AGE

•

MIDDLETOWN FIRM LOANED
STATE MONEY TO EXPAND

•

FENCING IN YOUR SWIMMING POOL
CAN SAVE A CHILD'S LIFE

•

PRESS TOURS RAVAGED CITY

•

GOVERNMENT TO BAN
BALDNESS, SEX DRUGS

•

POLICE ARREST 59 DISABLED IN PROTEST

•

PROGRESS SLOW IN BEATING DEATH

•

MOUNTIES CHARGE TRUDEAU'S EX-WIFE

•

DEAN OF MEN, DEAN OF WOMEN
PROMISE TO STOP DRINKING ON CAMPUS

Often the problem is one of word order and the
relationships among words. When a Canadian newspaper announced, **BLIND WOMAN FORCED BY
COPS TO CLEAN UP AFTER HER GUIDE DOG
ACCEPTS SETTLEMENT,** readers were left scratch-
ing their heads and trying to figure out whether it
was the woman or the dog who negotiated. All it
takes is one grammatical slip, and zap! the presses
spit out fifty thousand copies of the late edition, each
paper containing a headline like these:

ACID RAIN LINKED TO EMISSIONS
BY REAGAN'S AIDE

•

MAN FOUND BEATEN, ROBBED BY POLICE

•

CEMETERY ALLOWS PEOPLE
TO BE BURIED BY THEIR PETS

•

PHONE WORKER CITED
FOR HELPING HURT WOMAN

•

HUB OFFICER SHOT
AFTER STOPPING CAR
RELEASED FROM HOSPITAL

•

KICKING BABY CONSIDERED
TO BE HEALTHY

•

DIRECTOR OF TRUMAN LIBRARY KNOWS
NEWSMAN'S PROBLEMS—HE WAS ONE

•

**ATTORNEYS GO ALONG
WITH STRIKING WORKERS**

•

DAD WANTS BABY LEFT IN AIRPLANE

•

**NEW HOUSING FOR WORKERS
NOT YET DEAD**

•

**RUNAWAY KILLED BY GUNMAN
BURIED IN PAUPER'S GRAVE**

•

MAN TRYING TO GET KITE ELECTROCUTED

•

**EX-FEMALE UMP FILES
SEX DISCRIMINATION CHARGE**

•

**SUDDEN RUSH TO HELP
PEOPLE OUT OF WORK**

•

**HOUSE DECLARED HAUNTED
BY A MANHATTAN APPEALS COURT**

You would think that the reporters who wrote the stories would also write the headlines, but that would be too easy. The creators of headlines are usually copy editors who, with time constantly hanging over their heads, must often give the story a cursory look. This separation of writer and headline-maker

sometimes causes readers to throw up their hands
and exclaim, "huh?" because of headlines that lack
anything in the way of apparent logic:

SERIOUS CRIME DOWN,
BUT MURDERS INCREASE

•

6 FOUND SLAIN IN MIAMI;
MISSING TODDLER SOUGHT

•

RICHARD BURTON FACES SURGERY
ON HIS BACK

•

ALDERMEN ACCEPT REFUSE PAYMENT

•

FRIED CHICKEN COOKED
IN MICROWAVE WINS TRIP

•

ANOTHER BODY FOUND MISSING

•

WOMAN COMMITS SUICIDE, SETS CAR AFIRE

•

MAN ROBS, THEN KILLS HIMSELF

•

TWO TEENAGERS INDICTED
FOR DROWNING IN LAKE

•

NUDE MAN PULLS KNIFE ON WORKERS

•

COPS QUIZ VICTIM IN FATAL SHOOTING

•

DEATH OF BETTE DAVIS
BRINGS FLOOD OF PRAISE

•

A GRATEFUL NATION BURIES SAM RAYBURN

•

DRUGS AND CRIME ARE OVERRATED

•

PHILADELPHIA AIMS AT ILLITERACY

•

DOVER CLINIC APPLAUDS STATE'S
UNWANTED PREGNANCY DRIVE

•

PENNY NOT WORTH
A PLUG NICKEL ANY MORE

•

MAN SHOT, STABBED;
DEATH BY NATURAL CAUSES RULED

•

GIRL BECOMES METHODIST
AFTER DELICATE OPERATION

•

POLICE LOOK FOR SCREAMS IN THE NIGHT

Other headline howlers present a penetrating glimpse into the self-evident. Newspaper editors appear to be one slug short of a full sentence when they create headlines that blare the obvious:

MATH IMPROVEMENT INDICATES
LEARNING IS TIED TO TEACHING

•

ALEXANDER HOPING PAST IS BEHIND HIM

•

SCHOOL BOARD AGREES
TO DISCUSS EDUCATION

•

NEW BAR EXAM TO INCLUDE
TEST OF LEGAL SKILLS

•

HALF OF ALL CHILDREN
TESTED SCORED BELOW AVERAGE

•

TESTER LINKS PYGMY DEFECT
TO SHORTNESS

•

DEATH PENALTY SAID TO BE DEBASING

•

MISSOURI GAS CHAMBER IS UNSAFE

•

MURDER BY COMPANIONS AFFECTS
INMATE'S CHANCE FOR PAROLE

Sextra! Sextra!

As you saw in the last chapter, one of the hazards of headline writing is the potential for unwitting and witless double entendres. When the extra meaning of the headline is suggestive, salacious, and sexy, the copy editor may wake up screaming in the night.

A Minneapolis newspaper story told about the distribution of Community Chest funds. The headline boasted, BIG CHEST IS AID TO GIRL SCOUTS.

An Illinois paper is credited with this World War II suggestion: WOMEN URGED TO CONSERVE MANPOWER BY USING BOYS.

A Manila woman, who worked for an American-owned tobacco company in the Philippines, was kidnapped by four men. The woman, twenty years of age, ran away from her abductors while they were asleep. Then she reported her travails to the *Manila Daily Mirror*, which ran this front page headline: GIRL EMPLOYEE BARES SNATCH.

Sports stories seem to be especially powerful magnets for pornographically punderful headlines. A Massachusetts paper covering a contract dispute between Oakland A's owner Charlie Finley and ex-manager Dick Williams blared, FINLEY WON'T RELEASE DICK. In its unbounded joy over the en-

Breast implants seized by marshals

try of marathoner Craig Virgin in the Independence Day Peachtree Classic, an Atlanta paper announced VIRGIN TO PROVIDE WEEKEND EXCITEMENT.

On the morning of the Illinois-Ohio State football game when Illinois would be playing without the services of its star running back, Frosty Peters, a newspaper published this beauty: ILLINI FACE BUCKS WITH FROSTY PETERS OUT.

Back before World War II, the conservative *Saturday Evening Post* ran an article written by the wife of a billiards professional. She told how part of her job as her husband's assistant was seeing that all was in order for his exhibitions. Among her duties, she had to make sure that the billiard balls were exactly at room temperature.

The *Post*'s makeup editor decided that a subhead was needed here, so he wrote: SHE KEEPS HIS BALLS WARM. Nearly a million copies had gone out before someone woke up.

Here are some more screamers, too bizarrely lewd, lascivious, and licentious to have been published purposely in family newspapers:

ANTI-NUDITY LAW TO GET CLOSER LOOK

•

FLASHER CASE NEARLY WRAPPED UP,
CAMPUS POLICE SAY

•

HEALTH INSURERS SHOULD
COVER NEW BREASTS

•

ARGUS MAKES OFFER
TO SCREW CO. STOCKHOLDERS

●

FEMALE POLITICIANS TO DISCUSS
SACRIFICES, JOYS OF PUBIC SERVICE

●

COLUMBUS DISCOVERED VIRGINS
AND THEY ARE STILL FASCINATING

●

FORMER STATE TROOPER LOSES
APPEAL IN SEX CASE

●

EASTERN PILOTS MOUNT PICKETS
AT AIRPORT

●

WOMAN TO DROP SUIT FOR SPERM

●

WOMEN SOUGHT FOR STATE POLICE

●

VENEREAL DISEASE IS LINKED TO CRACK

●

PRO BALLER DIES IN BED

●

BLOODY BUTT HURTS RAMIREZ

●

BEAUTY QUEEN UNVEILS BUST
AT DEDICATION CEREMONY

●

FATHER OF 9 FINED $100
FOR FAILING TO STOP

•

MASSIVE ORGAN DRAWS CROWDS

•

TWO RECRUITS SATISFY
ESU WOMEN'S COACH

•

DO-IT-YOURSELF PREGNANCY KIT
TO GO ON SALE

•

RHODE ISLAND SECRETARY
EXCITES FURNITURE EXPERTS

•

ON-THE-JOB SEX HARASSMENT
RESPONSIBILITY OF EMPLOYEES

•

PEOPLE SHOULD EVACUATE
WHEN GAS ODOR PRESENT

•

L. I. STIFFENS FOR CONNIE'S BLOW

•

SPERMICIDE MAKER SCORED

•

LAWMAKERS HOPE TO PASS WATER,
OTHER BILLS IN TRENTON

•

PETROLEUM JELLY KEEPS
IDLE TOOLS RUST-FREE

●

BREAST IMPLANTS SEIZED BY MARSHALS

What may be the most titillating typographical misfortune ever appeared in the *Green Bay Press-Gazette*. The paper was caught with its Freudian slip showing in its headline for a front-page item on Wisconsin governor Tommy Thompson. The story reported that the governor was in the process of vetoing a record number of items proposed in the state budget, and the headline read: THOMPSON'S PENIS A SWORD.

Incorrect Corrections

It is a small miracle that newspapers have so few typographical errors, considering the pressure of deadlines and the number of people who handle each piece of copy. When newspapers attempt to correct the mistakes that occasionally slither in, the results can go awry.

One Monday, not long ago, the following classified classic ran in a small-town newspaper:

FOR SALE: R. D. Jones has one sewing machine for sale. Phone 948-0707 after 7 p.m. and ask for Mrs. Kelly, who lives with him cheap.

Now watch what happened to the attempts to repair the damage:

(Tuesday) NOTICE—We regret having erred in R. D. Jones' ad yesterday. It should have read: One sewing machine for sale. Cheap. Phone 948-0707 and ask for Mrs. Kelly, who lives with him after 7 p.m.

(Wednesday) NOTICE—R. D. Jones has informed us that he has received several annoying telephone calls because of an error we made in his classified ad yesterday. His ad should read as follows: FOR SALE: R. D. Jones has one sewing machine for sale.

Apology: I originally wrote, "Woodrow Wilson's wife grazed sheep on the front lawn of the White House." I'm sorry typesetting inadvertently left out the word *sheep*.

Cheap. Phone 948-0707 7 p.m. and ask for Mrs. Kelly, who loves with him.

(Thursday) NOTICE: I, R. D. Jones, have no sewing machine for sale. I smashed it. Don't call 948-0707, as the telephone has been disconnected. I have NOT been carrying on with Mrs. Kelly. Until yesterday, she was my housekeeper, but she quit.

Clearly, there are times when it is best to leave well enough alone—or perhaps we should say leave bad enough alone, before it becomes worse:

- Middletown's annual Cherry Blossom Festival will be May 13 through 10. The event was incorrectly listed on a State-issued calendar for May.
- An item in Thursday's *Nation Digest* about Massachusetts' budget crisis made reference to new taxes that will help put Massachusetts "back in the African-American." The item should have said "back in the black."
- In Saturday's *Enterprise* an article on the Church of Jesus Christ of Latter-Day Saints—the Mormons—incorrectly said that 1.06 million members of the church live in Utah, "a state in which 70 percent take LSD." The article should have read "a state which is 70 percent LDS (Latter-Day Saints)."
- In one edition of today's Food Section, an inaccurate number of jalapeño peppers was given for Jeanette Crowley's Southwestern chicken salad recipe. The recipe should call for two, not 21, jalapeño peppers.
- Apology: I originally wrote, "Woodrow Wilson's wife grazed sheep on the front lawn of the White House." I'm sorry typesetting inadvertently left out the word *sheep*.
- CLARIFICATION. The phrase "Dummy Head,"

which was accidentally printed beneath a photograph in Thursday's *Clarion-Dispatch* was intended as a typographical notation for use in the production process. It was not intended to describe in any way the subject of the photograph.

- Due to a telephonic error in transmission we stated yesterday that Mr. Roger Cranwell will be knighted next month. In fact, he will be 90 next month.

- In Thursday's editorial on Assembly District 24, the word *treatment* was left out of a sentence about candidate Ken Baker. It should have said that Baker "cautiously supports substance-abuse treatment in prisons."

- CORRECTION: Because of a reporting error, an item in this column Sept. 3 incorrectly stated that Santa Clara County Bar Association member Eugene Karlov was called a "Nazi" by a fellow bar member. Karlov was called a "communist." We regret the error.

- Sister Mary's "bust clinic" referred to last month was, of course, a "busy clinic."

- In an effort to make amends for the appearance of too many typos in the printing of Joanne Timmons's piece in the last issue of this magazine, a corrected version is herewith presented.

- CORECTION: . . .

- CORRECTION: In an article run June 28 on the Bailey College commencement speaker Peace Corps Director Mariette Donnelly, it was reported that she urged graduates to actively engage in "global riotism." Due to a computer error, this was a misquote. It should have read that Donnelly urged graduates to engage in "global patriotism."

Words That Don't Ad Up

Advertising is more important than most people realize. American advertisers spend more than $50 billion a year to ensure that the average American family reads, sees, and hears about a thousand commercial messages a day. What we eat, drink, wear, drive, read, watch, listen to, and live in depends largely on ads.

Before the invention of printing, sellers hired people to run through the streets shouting the virtues of their wares. Nowadays we have newspapers and magazines to do the job. But sometimes advertisements in print are fraught with ad-versity. As certain classified classics demonstrate, it's an ad, ad, ad, ad world out there:

- The Macon County Humane Society offers a free spay/neutering to senior citizens if they adopt an animal out of the animal shelter. Be sure the gift of a pet is a welcome gift.
- Remember, you get what you pay for. And at Hub Furniture Store, you pay less.
- Home. $199,500. Great Location. ⅔'s of an acre with 4 bedrooms, 2-bath, brick Cape. Built the way they used to. Won't last.

Why not have the kids shot for Easter, or have a family portrait taken? What have you to lose?

- We are proud of the part we have played in the tremendous growth of our city.—Valley Mattress
- Prevent damage to garden and lawns from burrowing rodents with the electronic stake that emits vibration and sound that's intensely annoying to underground rodents up to 100 feet in diameter.
- Try our cough syrup. You will never get any better.
- Images, Inc., is the place where romance novelist Danielle Steel rolls off the press.
- Why not have the kids shot for Easter, or have a family portrait taken? What have you to lose?
- Our dish detergent produces a higher degree of spotlessness.
- Marsden Park is the biggest park of its size in Central North Dakota.
- FOR SALE: Pair Holstein oxen, 3200 lbs, 8 years old, with horns capped by local blacksmith with brass balls.
- FOR SALE: Bull dog. Will eat anything. Loves children.
- FOR SALE: 9-volt smoke alarm with silencer.
- MUST SELL: 3 grave spaces in Laureland, very reasonable. Plus air-conditioner.
- MUST SELL: Health food store, due to failing health.
- FOR SALE: Instant coffee table.
- FOR SALE: Used girl's bicycle (and the likes of a gorgeous man's ring, a green girl's coat, an old baby's carriage, a large woman's purse, an old-fashioned girl's wagon, a plaid man's jacket, 2 used men's snowmobile helmets, an unused woman's fur coat).
- FOR SALE: Hunting Camp. Completely furnished. Assessable year round.

- FOR SALE: Gent's upright urinal; also microphone, stand, and amplifier.
- LOST. 2-year-old brown male Datsun, very well behaved and friendly.
- *On a hospital bulletin board:* The Community Chorus will begin Monday night rehearsals at 6 p.m. We have special need for men's voices, but all parts are welcome.
- Grafton County's only full-sized community newspaper! Disturbing to over 18,000 households per week!
- FOR RENT. Bridal suite. Adults only.
- FOR RENT. Front room, suitable for two ladies, use of kitchen or two gentlemen.
- FOR RENT. Fully furnished house. Includes three toilets. $200 per wee.
- FORECLOSURE SALE: 2 Story 8 Room Saltbox Home With 3.48 Acres of Land & Panasonic Views
- PART-TIME HELP WANTED. Must have creative skills, drivers license, and car with outgoing personality.
- CLASSIFIED: An unexpected vacancy for a knife-thrower's assistant. Rehearsals start immediately.
- ARE YOUR TALENTS BEING WASTED? . . . You could be selected to manage small tasks, make beds, pass water . . .
- AUTOMATIC BLANKET Ensure sound sleep with one of our dealers.
- GIVE US YOUR DIRTY CLOTHES Ladies! If you drive by our new launderette and drop off your clothes, you will receive very special attention!
- CARVEL ACADEMY In beautiful New Hampshire. Coeducational. Special openings for boys.
- Monadnock Hospice: For patients who need help facing death and their loved ones.

- WANTED: A mahogany living room table, by a lady with Heppelwhite legs.
- WANTED: Self-storing aluminum window salesman.
- WANTED: Medical Analist.
- WANTED: ELECTRIC KILN for school, big enough for 40 children.
- WANTED: Large public hospital seeking a Risk Manager/Patient Affairs Coordinator to direct program including patient grievance systems and decadent affairs.
- WANTED: Animal Shelter Manager. . . . Salary commiserate with experience.
- WANTED BY MACHINE TOOL FACTORY: Male parts handlers.
- WANTED: Woman to share apt. w/ washer and dryer.
- WANTED: Dishes. Especially Currier and Ives bowels.
- NOW ACCEPTING applications for cooks between 2 and 5.
- HAVE FAMILY, would like to exchange for home in Amsterdam.
- Elderly woman seeks female to share house & perform cleaning & some nursing assistance. Must be a nonsmoker & drinker.
- EXTREMELY INDEPENDENT MALE. 17 years old, needs to rent room. Call his mother at . . .
- 2 YEAR old teacher needed. 9–6. Experience required.
- SECRETARIAL / CLERICAL—Excellent word processing & typing skills. Conscious, creative and detail oriented.
- AVAILABLE. French speaking secretary who speaks floorless English.
- AVAILABLE. Work Skills: Strong on interper-

- sonal relationships, typing, filing, and reproduction.
- Doctor, 50 years old, wants to meet beautiful SWF, 23–29, to spoil and share the good things of life.
- Cleaning services. We do condos, offices, and residents.
- 3-room apt. incl. heat, hot water, stove, refrig., smoke alarm, single female.
- Facilities include two tennis courts, an 18-hole swimming facility, and a health club.
- Typewriter: works for only $10.
- Nobody Can Beat Our Meat.
- Reputed Eating Place and Coffee Shoppe.
- Artie's Restaurant and Yogurt Parlor: "An Alternative to Good Eating."
- FOR SALE: Braille dictionary. Must see to appreciate! Call Jerry.
- There is no electricity (no heat or bathroom) in the Meeting House (1772). A portable toilet will be available to the right of the building. Seating is somewhat limited.
- *In an ad for an oak bookcase:* Simple assembly, requiring only a flat-head and Phillips screwdriver.
- This clothing is designed for breaking wind and repelling water.
- The mating dance of the sandhill crane is a sight never to be forgotten. You will be led by a professional wildlife biologist who is also a dedicated birdwatcher.
- 10 FREE French Fry Certificates for only $1.00.
- 4:15 PM. PHIL DONAHUE; 60 min. Scheduled topic: suicide. (Live)
- *Ad for a "Blue Hawaii Beach party":* Free lays to the first 50 people.
- No detail too small to overlook.

- Springer Spaniel female whose owner desires to mate w/beautiful male, liver & white springer thoroughbred with AKC papers.
- *In a dentist's notice regarding periodontal care:* When we ask you to come in more often, it is likely you have deep pockets.
- ATTENTION: All Petites. Enter the most promising Petite Model contest. No talent or modeling experience required.
- ATTENTION: new mothers, grandparents, baby shoes bronzed or personalized.
- Now you can borrow enough money to get completely out of debt.
- Inflation Got Your $Dollars$? Munroe & Sons Constructed Homes Can Give You Quality At Tomorrow's Prices.
- St. Petersburg Opera Company, Inc., presents THE MIKADO, by Gilbert & Sullivan. Sung in English.
- Channel 16 temporarily off the air due to technical improvements.
- New England Embroidery purses featuring Loons designed by Ann Webster and other native birds.
- Imagine sensational recipes that take you step-by-step through every dish.
- Buy 6, get 2!
- *On the menu of a Chinese restaurant:* We serve dead shrimp on warm vegetables with a smile.
- *From a request for a magazine subscription renewal:* Dear recently-expired subscriber: . . .

�֎ IV ✤
The Tower of Babble

A sports jacket may be worn to dinner, but not trousers.

Global Gabble

When you toast in a foreign language, caution is advised. Otherwise you may end up like the Middle Eastern oil mogul who lifted his glass, looked his American lady companion in the eye, and said with dignity, "Well . . . up yours!"

If you are writing bilingual guidebooks, try to avoid instructions like those to tourists visiting a French château. The French admonition to avoid trespassing in the master bedroom was translated into English as: "Please do not invade Madame's private parts."

If you are editing the newsletter of a multinational corporation, try to nip in the bud gaffes like "We extend special respect to Mrs. Jamison, whose unique capabilities are truly ignobling."

If you are publishing a children's book, try not to use the title *A Big Cock and a Leaking Mouth*. A Shanghai company did and offered this advertising blurb for the story: "It is a bad habit for children to have a meal walking about with a rice bowl and dripping grains of rice here and there. This colour picture story book of children's life is written down for the purpose of helping the children to get rid of this bad habit. The illustrations visually express the contents with plenty of children's interest and temperament."

What we actually see in *A Big Cock and a Leaking Mouth* is a picture of a little boy with a rice bowl, and a large rooster eating the leaking ("spilt") rice.

English is the most widely spoken language in history. More than half of English-speakers did not hear the language as babies and did not grow up speaking it as children—and this community of second-language speakers of English is growing more rapidly than that of native users.

English is also widely misspoken and miswritten. English may be the international language of travel, but the English-speaking traveler is often asked to chew on menu offerings like these: whores dover, white whine, cock and tail, soap of the day, buff steak, prostitude hams, hambugger, spaghetti fungus, dreaded veel cutlets, foul breast, muscles in sailor's sauce, hen fried with butler, prawns in spit, utmost of chicken with smashed pot, muchrooms, mushed potatoes, backed beans, raped carrots, cabitch, groin salad, lemon jews, and Turkey coffee.

English may be the international language of business, but a number of notices and notes, observed in various hotels and other establishments, suggest a veritable Tower of Babble:

In a Polish restaurant: As for the tripe served you at the Hotel Monopol, you will be singing its praises to your grandchildren on your deathbed.

In a Parisian restaurant: We serve five o'clock tea at all hours.

In a Bangkok watering hole: The Shadiest Cocktail Bar in Bangkok.

At the entrance to a hotel swimming pool on the French Riviera: Swimming is forbidden in the absence of a savior.

At a Sri Lankan pool: Do not use the diving board when the swimming pool is empty.

In a Torremolinos hotel: We highly recommend the hotel tart.

In a small Ionian Sea hotel: In order to prevent shoes from misleying, please don't corridor them. The Management of this Hotel cannot be held.

In a Tel Aviv hotel room: If you wish for breakfast, lift the telephone and our waitress will arrive. This will be enough to bring your food up.

In a Belgrade hotel: Let us know about any inficiency as well as leaking on the service.

In an Istanbul hotel room: To call the room service, please open the door and call Room Service.

In a Havana hotel: Guests are prohibited from walking around the lobby in large groups in the nude.

In a Beirut hotel: Ladies are kindly requested not to have their babies in the cocktail bar.

In a Cairo bar: Unaccompanied ladies not admitted unless with husband or similar.

In a Japanese hotel: We now have a Sukiyaki Restaurant with lodging facilities for those who want have experiences on Japanese bedding.

In a Mexico City hotel: We sorry to advise you that by a electric disperfect in the generator master of the elevator we have the necessity that don't give service at our distinguishable guests.

In an Ankara hotel: Please hang your order before retiring on your doorknob.

In a hotel on the Gaspé Peninsula: No dancing in the bathrooms!

In a Madrid hotel: If you wish disinfection, enacted in your presence, cry out for the chambermaid.

On a Tokyo elevator: Keep your hands away from unnecessary buttons for you.

Two from the same hotel in Paris: A sports jacket may be worn to dinner, but not trousers. And: Tea in a bag, just like mother.

Chinese road sign: Go soothingly on the greasy mud, for therein lurks the skid demon.

Midnight sign-off on a French radio station: We hope you have enjoyed our nocturnal emissions and will be with us for more tomorrow.

In an ad for a Mexico City restaurant: Dance to violin music while you overlook a fascinating view of the city.

In the window of a Barcelona travel agency: Go away.

On a plastic toy manufactured in Hong Kong: Plastic Bugs. Scare Your Friends. Put Them in a Drink. They Float.

On an amusement park ride in Saudi Arabia: For your safety this game is not allowed for those who suffer from hearts, diabetics, nerves, high pressure, and pregnants.

At a Budapest zoo: Please do not feed the animals. If you have suitable food, give it to the guard on duty.

In the window of a Swedish furrier: Fur coats made for ladies from their own skins.

A Zanzibar barbershop window message: Gentlemen's throats cut with nice sharp razors.

At an Israeli butcher shop: I slaughter myself twice daily.

In a Vale of Kashmir bakery: First-class English loafer.

Headline in an Ethiopian newspaper: FORD, REAGAN NECK IN PRESIDENTIAL PRIMARY.

Ad in a Hong Kong newspaper: A dynamic mineral trading company has the following immediate position: FEMALE ASS MERCHANDISER.

Two highway signs in India: Avoid Overspeeding.
And: Always Avoid Accidents.

Sign in a Chinese restaurant bathroom: Employee
must wash your hands after each use.

*On various signs, packages, T-shirts, and shopping
bags in Japan:*

- Just Fit For You, King Kong
- Ease Your Bosoms
- Fancy Pimple
- Snow Is Popsy
- Persistent Pursuit of Dainty
- Vigorous Throw-Up
- A drop of sweat is the precious gift for your guts
- Tonight's the Bitch!

Ultimately, it is to Italy that we must turn for truly
inspired gibberish. Consider these instructions grac-
ing a packet of Italian convenience food: "Besmear
a backing pan, previously buttered with good tomato
sauce and after, dispose the cannelloni, lightly dis-
tanced between them in a only couch."

Or take these gems from Italian hotels and restaurants:

- If service is required, give two strokes to the
  maid and three to the waiter (sign over a bedside
  bell to be rung for service).
- It is kindly requested from our guests that they
  avoid dirting and doing rumours in the rooms.
- Hot and cold water running up and down the
  stairs.
- Be pleased to come lie down with our masseuse.
  She will make you forget all your tired.
- Please pay the house waiter the price of your
  consummation.
- Guests are advised that all fruits served have

been washed in water passed by the management.

In some Italian restaurants, the owner may include a personal message on the menu: "Offering my honored guests delicious meals as well as selected beverages is my endeavor served by well-trained waiters. Every readiness and efficiency to obtain this target is essential. Kind assist me in this task by taking at least one meal a day at my place where my specialty is pig."

Here is a selection of fire regulations in an Italian hotel:

IN BURNING CASE

1. The foredisposed ring bells for the adverting have a very strong sound and shall be actioned with breaks of one or two seconds between one ring and the other.

4. If the burning is in your room or around, and you think that has not been noted, advice immediatly the hotel staff.

5. If the burning has come in a part of your gangway, get wet abundantly a sheet then wrap it around yourself starting from your head then pass through quickly the danger area till you join the stairs.

6. If the flames or the intensly smoke prevent you to go away from your room and join the stairs, lean out from the balcony or the window and wait for the helps.

As a curtain call, I offer an "English" synopsis of Acts 1 and 4 of *Carmen* exactly as it appeared in the program for a recent performance of the opera in Genoa, Italy:

Act I. Carmen is a cigar-makeress from a tabago factory who loves with Don José of the mounting guard. Carmen takes a flower from her corsets and lances it to Don José (Duet: "Talk me of my mother"). There is a noise inside the tabago factory and the revolting cigar-makeresses burst into the stage. Carmen is arrested and Don José is ordered to mounting guard her but Carmen subduces him and he lets her escape.

Act 4. A place in Seville. Procession of balls-fighters, the roaring of the balls is heard in the arena. Escamillio enters (Aria and chorus: "Toreador, Toreador, All Hail the Balls of a Toreador"). Enter Don José (Aria: "I Do Not Threaten. I besooch you"). But Carmen repels him wants to join with Escamillio now chaired by the crowd. Don José stabbs her (Aria: "Oh Rupture, Rupture, You May Arrest Me. I Did Kill Her") he sings, "Oh my beautiful Carmen, my subductive Carmen."

Two signs wonderfully sum up the state of international English: A placard in a Mexico City shop proclaims, "Broken English spoken perfectly," and a sign above the door of a Parisian bistro announces, "More or less we speak English." The fact that the speaking of broken English is more than less adds a bit of unscheduled fun to a visit abroad.

Mix Jell-O as directed on box. Sit in refrigerator for about a half hour till it starts to gel. Then add cottage cheese and crushed pineapple.

Simply Follow Instructions

Cautionary advice posted on a Russian ship helpfully explained, "Helpsavering apparata in emergings behold many whistles! Associate the stringing apparata about the bosoms and meet behind. Flee then to the indifferent lifesaving shippen obediencing the instructs of the vessel chief."

Spectators for a motoring event on the French Riviera were enlightened with this explanation: "Competitors will defile themselves on the promenade at 11 A.M., and each car will have two drivers who will relieve themselves at each other's convenience."

The instructions in foreign lands are quite instructive. The most loopy, wifty, and wiggy directives are those for assembling and using products manufactured abroad and exported to English-speaking customers. One classic is the label on the back of a retractable multipurpose "Touch-Knife" manufactured in Osaka, Japan. The package simply says, "Caution: Blade Extremely Sharp! Keep Out of Children."

Here is my personal directory of misdirected directions that get lost in translation:

Accompanying a computer modem made in Taiwan: Once you have the necessary items, plug the

RS-232 connector on the back side of the Mini Modem 2400 into the RS-232C connector on your computer, printer, or terminal, then screw them.

On an electronic mosquito repeller manufactured in Taiwan: Exposion to the direct rays of the sun for a long time may shorten the life of battery.

In case of outdoor, usses in a boat, under bench, inside of tent will be preferable.

If without special frequency, some similar mosquitos repeller which will invite to gather mosquitos. Please adjust frequency at once if above phenomenon.

Use special frequency and biological research to driving them, the sonic wave is harmless for human beings and pets so could used by continuous. But stop to use it for a while is the sick man or user is sensitive to sound.

On the box of an alarm clock made in Taiwan: Thank you to perfection of alarming mechanism. You are never awake when you are sleeping.

For a Japanese-manufactured "Turning Type Pencil": Please to use in accordance with our instructions for this pencil is quite new in that a particular idea has been employed in its nib, so that you write with fluent by simply adjusting it.

Conclusion: In the instruction of this patented product, if there is anything not mentioned completely, please operate by comparing with the picture. May all users write fluently having immediate success with one pencil in hand.

On the box containing a battery manufactured in Taiwan: Pack your battery, after assembled, please put it more powerfully at first times.

Instructions for assembling a step stool made in Taiwan: Step 1: When you want to open and use it, don't put your hand on the end of up step board and down step, you must be put your hands on the fore leg and back leg that between of down cross bar and seat leg.

OK! Opening that's right.

Step 2: When you want to take to the other place, pushing the plate spring with your hand of one, holding the belt with the other hand, take up the step stool with holding the belt hand.

OK! You are success!

On the back of a box containing a musical doorbell, made in Hong Kong:

SAVING ENERGY: We can save the electrical expenses in a family by using no electricity.

IT IS STILL AT WORK WHILE SHORTING: It will not be affected by short, as to lose ring-bell efficacy.

AUDIO-DESIGN; It is adopted from the piano-music with beautiful and graceful sound.

INSTALLING IT EASILY AND SIMPLY: At the back side of the musical bell there is a paper sticker, we can install it by ourselves without sending for electrician.

NOBLE AND GRACEFUL WALL-DESIGN: Being designed beautifully, when we decorate it in our living-room, and it is noble and graceful style.

AVOIDING ELECTRICAL DANGERS AND DAMAGE: Using the electricity of household electric products, the wire easily catches fire. In this bad condition, the "Nonelectric Musical Bell" can make up the weakness.

I am told that foreign manufacturers are beginning to hire better translators to write their instructions.

How unfortunate.

Before you sneer too meanly, know that we in the good old U.S. of A. can also create havoc when we try to communicate in other languages. On the San Jose Public Library appeared a $10,000 sign extending greetings to patrons in twenty-seven languages. Unfortunately, the message in Tagalog included the word *tuley*, instead of *tuloy*, altering the meaning from "welcome" to "circumcision." In the Sky Harbor Airport in Phoenix, a sign proclaiming drinking age in Arizona omitted the tilde over the word *año*, so that the word "year" became "anus."

Other instructions that have all been made right here in America do not involve translation errors but simply a slaughtering of the King's and Queen's English:

On a warranty certificate: To preserve your Rusty Jones warranty on your car upholstery, you must pick up a canister of fluid and spray it on yourself.

Sign on a toilet paper rack: Pull down and tear up.

Label on cough syrup: Hold one teaspoon in mouth for five minutes and expectorate for five to seven days.

On a postcard: In order that we may continue to serve you without interruption, we hope you will favor us with a remittance for continuing your subscription before your expiration date.

Note on a package of frozen peas: MICROWAVE INSTRUCTIONS: Place contents of package in covered glass casserole, add 2 tablespoons water. Cook on high setting for 3 minutes. Stir and cook on high setting another 1 to 12 minutes. [If the casserole is covered, how can anything be put into it?]

On a mix package: Combine all ingredients except the bananas. Mix well and sit in the refrigerator.

Similarly on a Jell-O box: Mix Jell-O as directed on box. Sit in refrigerator for about a half hour till it starts to gel. Then add cottage cheese and crushed pineapple.

On a box containing a screwdriver with a small flashlight built into the handle: Now you can see what you're screwing in the dark.

Figuratively Misspeaking

A professor once asked his teenage son, "What's a metaphor?"

"For cows to graze in," the boy replied.

The young man is far from being the only one to mix up his figures of speech. After engaging in a debate at Dartmouth College's Baker Library, then-presidential candidate George Bush was asked by reporters if he felt like a winner, or just a survivor. Bush replied, "I don't think I hit anything out of the ball park, but I don't think they laid a glove on me either."

Bush himself has admitted that "fluency in English is something that I'm often not accused of." As president, he responded to a reporter's question about his role in the Iran-Contra affair with this mixed-up metaphor: "You're burning up time. The meter is running through the sand on you." In an effort to encourage an optimistic outlook, Bush lost another battle with a standard metaphor when he beseeched an audience: "Please just don't look at part of the glass, the part that is only less than half full."

When asked in a TV interview about the resignation of Chief of Staff John Sununu, Vice President Dan Quayle replied, "This isn't a man who is leaving

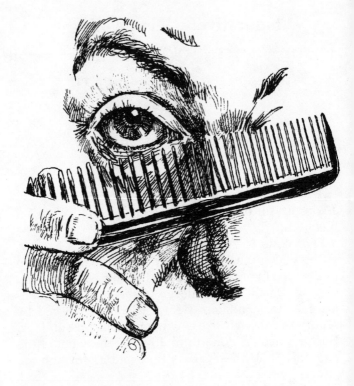

From now on, I'm watching everything you do with a fine-tooth comb.

with his head between his legs." Now there's a vice president who has a good tail on his shoulders.

Republicans aren't the only ones who can be anatomically incorrect. Many a metaphor has been miscegenated bipartisanly. Democratic presidential hopeful Jerry Brown, for example, referred to campaign cash as "the umbilical cord that . . . every major politician in this country still sucks on."

Budget Committee chairman Jim Sasser is said to have said, "This thing could sprout wings and become an irresistible political juggernaut that will thunder through the halls of Congress like a rolling locomotive."

A New Hampshire congressman once observed, "What the people of this state deserve is clean, fresh, wholesome pasteurized milk. And I'm going to the State House and take the bull by the horns until we get it."

A Canadian M.P. lamented, in classical fashion, "When we opened Pandora's box, out came a Trojan horse," while a veteran cog in a municipal political machine created this beauty with more honesty than he could have known: "Don't rock the trough." It's enough to make your head stand on end, according to one mixed metaphor heard on the floor of the Wisconsin State Senate.

"You're mixing apples and orange juice!" a Capitol Hill pol once exclaimed in the heat of blather. While we bear in mind that language is what separates the human beings from the politicians, we must also realize that politics isn't the only arena for miscegenated metaphors and fractured figures:

- It's time to belly up to the bar and lay the cards on the table.
- We have buttered our bread, and now we have to lie on it.

- From now on, I'm watching everything you do with a fine-tooth comb.
- We want to be sure our dominoes are all lined up the same way before anyone comes in to rattle our cage.
- This sign thing could be the stickiest wicket in the whole municipal bag of worms.
- My husband just got laid off, so please keep your ear to the grindstone for us.
- He's the type who'll cut your throat behind your back.
- She's such a pain in the ass. She's an albatross around my neck.
- When you get down to square tacks . . .
- He threw a hundred pitches in six innings, and that's a mouthful.
- Don't throw the garbage out with the bathwater.
- Once you let the horse out of the barn, it's hard to get it back in again. It snowballs and has a life of its own, kind of like a computer virus.
- The White House advisers to Mr. Nixon thought that the scientists were using science as a sledgehammer to grind their political axes.
- It was a case of the tail biting the dog.
- The issue is on the back burner in a holding pattern.
- Governor Corrigan says he doesn't want to "cry wolf in a crowded theater."
- Everything goes hand and foot together.
- We took the thunder out of his sails.
- He's been burning the midnight oil from both ends
- They're in a fix, they're in a pickle, they're on thin water, and they're pulling out all the punches.
- When you're the one who's getting it in the neck, it's a bitter pill to swallow.
- He's trying to get his foot in the tent.

- He pulled the wool right out from under my feet.
- He hit the nail right on the jackpot.
- Just wait until the shoe falls on the other foot.
- The project is going to pot in a hand basket in one full sweep.
- If we don't watch out, they'll pull the rug out from under us in midstream.
- When he finds out what we've done, the sparks will hit the fan.
- The problem was small, but it was baseballing.
- They were raking him over the ropes.
- We can shoot potholes in that argument.
- He's flying against the current.
- People are dying like hotcakes.
- You can't get blood from a tulip.
- The man was drunk to the bone.
- It's as easy as falling off a pie.
- "I would not have gone over my dead body," the woman said of the ceremony.
- He's a little green behind the ears.
- He's up the tree without a paddle.
- It turned out to be one of those red herrings around our necks.
- We'll burn that bridge when we come to it.
- Don't kiss a gift horse in the mouth.
- He said it would be a boost in the arm for the nation's teachers.
- It would take only ten minutes if you could walk as the crow flies.
- Oregon is on the cutting edge of decline.
- And this is only a chip off the iceberg.
- Varney lit the spark that turned the tide in the ball game.
- The crowd was sitting on the edge of their tenter-hooks.
- The pendulum in this game is swinging back and forth like a metronome.

- [Magic] Johnson's three field goals have taken the sails out of the crowd.
- The crowd is making its way to its feet.
- It turned out to be one of those red herrings around our necks.
- He wanted to make it clear that he was not speaking through rose-colored glasses.
- Stop speaking off the top of your hat.
- Life isn't always a bowl of chili.
- We can't just sit on our duff and rest on our laurels anymore.
- IDG and Ziff Publishing were said to be sharpening their swords for a shoot-out.
- "We've got talent here, but we obviously need some shoring up in several positions depthwise," he said. "This year we have to do a lot of weeding out and see what cream comes to the top."
- She took to it like a duck out of water.
- You can't go there cold turkey with egg on your face.
- You're on gravy street.
- The barometer is skyrocketing down to 3 degrees F.
- There's so much going on at work, I can barely keep my feet above water.
- That was before jealousy reared its ugly claws.
- She looks like death swarmed over.
- To exclude the evidence would be like shutting the door after the cat has run out.
- I took the threats with a grain of sand.
- The program will allow us to start a new leaf.
- It was his death knoll.
- He's going to have to tread water lightly.
- I got caught in the web of a cross fire.
- I don't want to jump the gun and be left out on a limb.
- It sounds like a can of worms to me.

- Passengers like to shop at airports. Our research has shown that shoes are especially popular. Shoe Mart sells more shoes per square foot than it does in any of its other stores.

Right after the start of the Palestinian uprising, an English-language tourism advertisement in Europe touted the benefits of visiting Israel. It cited the short distances involved in traveling therein, noting that "Jerusalem is just a stone's throw from Tel Aviv." The ad was hastily withdrawn.

For years, professors at Brown University have chuckled over and passed around this figurative mishmash culled from a Western Civilization exam: "The poet Dante stood with one foot firmly planted in the Middle Ages while with the other he saluted the rising dawn of the Renaissance."

After more than thirty years of collecting figures of speech that don't add up, I am able to present my choices for most blunderful metaphors of all time. Most of these examples are malaphors, attempted metaphors in which the comparison clashes shockingly with the content of the given statement:

- People who oppose abortion are laboring under a misconception.
- A trucker called to thank all of the courteous Seattle drivers he had run across.
- End-of-Summer Blowout Sale (tire ad in *Car and Driver*).
- "Our relief pitching was damned good, great," said manager Whitey Herzog, who violated a sacred cow for the second time in a week and got away with it.
- Dora was pleased as punch to be chosen chairman of the refreshments committee.

- David Bowie is one of a dying breed who will live on forever.
- It is time for some straight talk about the gay liberation movement.
- The space docking went off without a hitch.
- Alcohol is not my cup of tea.
- The casualties from the missile attacks were astronomically low.
- It has clung to the bowels of my brain.
- McLaren Casket Co. is closed today but may re-open soon with a skeleton crew.
- Whether the hurricane's eye will travel to the west of us is all up in the air.
- I personally could not stand by and watch a child starve to death. I would give an arm and a leg to feed them.
- That summer I finally got my leg operated on, and what a relief. It had been hanging over my head for years.
- Director of Public Works Greg Paulsen has indicated that the landfill would have to be closed in 1989, although that is not set in cement.
- Urbanology is a virgin field pregnant with possibilities.
- Cambodia has launched a crash course to train more pilots.
- Brown told the group he'll be in his office now "burning the midnight oil from 9 a.m. to 9 p.m."
- Most health concerns about coffee are groundless.
- Bare-bones health plans are not selling.
- He's going to step down until he's back on his feet.—a radio commentator on Jimmy Swaggart's latest sex scandal.
- We all have ancestors, and in this series I will encourage you to dig up yours.
- My life made a 360-degree turn.

- We went to Patagonia in search of the giant sloth, but as the giant sloth doesn't exist, it seems to me to have been something of a wild goose chase.
- Fuel injection technology has won wide acclaim in all walks of racing circles.
- This is Britain's first ever women's medal in the World Rowing Championships. Yes, it's been a long time out there in the desert for our women rowers.
- Now only a skeleton staff remains at the British Embassy in Teheran, keeping a stiff upper lip.
- I have the feeling that later in life, it will come time to settle down, preferably with a beautiful blonde with cobalt eyes and a brain to match.
- I've got a mind like a steel sieve.
- The coach's popularity is at a high ebb.
- I am putting aside everything I can for my goose egg.
- A man found a new way to import ice from Alaska to California, where it is selling like hot cakes.
- Vandergoltz explained that his leaving was entirely his decision: "I'll be turning fifty next year, and this is all consistent with my very firmly held conviction that you need to have a fresh face in the saddle at least every ten years."
- Stephen Cox is off to see the Munchkins, the wonderful Munchkins of Oz. But he has no yellow brick road to follow in his search for the little people who greeted Dorothy in the 1939 film _The Wizard of Oz_.

  "It may not be easy to find some of them," said the writer in St. Louis. "I know there are some of them still living but they've sort of fallen into the woodwork."

Archie Bunker's word choice was "legionary."

Going Bonkers with Bunker

Back in January of 1971 (has it really been that long?) the landmark series *All in the Family* lit up the tubes of our television sets. Written by Norman Lear, the series, depicting a bigoted blue-collar worker and his family, attracted increasingly large audiences of viewers by presenting some very new elements for a situation comedy—realistic characters, mature themes, frank dialogue, and socially sensitive issues.

A great part of the show's success must be attributed to the personality and power of the main character as interpreted by the incomparable Carroll O'Connor. The series has so touched the hearts and minds of the American viewing public that the name Archie Bunker has entered our language as the label for a lovable blue-collar ignoramus.

In the grand tradition of William Shakespeare's Doll Tearsheet and Richard Sheridan's Mrs. Malaprop, and the modern school of Dizzy Dean, Samuel Goldwyn, Yogi Berra, and Howard Cosell, Archie Bunker is also renowned for unfailingly tripping over his tongue. His word choice is so "legionary" that hilarious fractures of vocabulary have come to be called Bunkerisms. To use the great man's "epaulet," the name Bunker and the humorously illiterate misuse of words are like "two peas in a pot." Trust me, that ain't no "science friction," no "frigment" of my imagination.

The field of health care is especially prone to Bunkerizing. Men and women across our nation are inflicted with migrating headaches, inflamed prostrate glands, smiling mighty Jesus (spinal meningitis), acute vagina attacks, swollen asteroids, sick-as-hell anemia, hideous (and Hyannis) hernias, swollen nymph glands, compacted wisdom teeth, romantic fever, heat prostitution, heretical diseases, cereal palsy, mental pause, itching of the virginia, and minstrel cramps while administrating.

Bothered by a recurrent rash on his arms, a man went to see a germatologist. Another decided to have a bisectomy. A third was admitted to the hospital because he was suffering from DDTs. After a heart attack, yet another man was said to be convulsing in expensive care.

A woman was fitted with an IOU and another received a tubular litigation. A baby was born with its biblical cord wrapped around its neck, while a teenager who had stopped breathing was given the Hemlock maneuver and then artificial insemination.

The nation's menus are a veritable treasure trove of Bunkerisms. Many a meal eaten out has started with wanton, spit pea, or gestapo soup. Other repasts have included sweat and sour chicken, sweet peace, a vegetable melody, French cruellers, and crocktails and canopies.

Bunkerisms are not just all in the family. One of the reasons why the Archie Bunker character is so appealing is that so many people we hear seem to speak like him, including many a politician. Vice President Dan Quayle informed a crowd that "Republicans understand the importance of bondage between parents and their children." On arriving at his party's 1992 convention in New York, Democratic National Committee chairman Ron Brown announced, "On behalf of all of you, I want to express my appreciation for this tremendously warm recession."

A United States senator bellowed, "What we have here is a series of allegations—and we do know about the allegators," while a Wisconsin Assembly majority leader announced, "PACS are very circumcised in what they can do. Er, circumscribed. Very limited."

A newspaper story reported that the conservative wing of the Republican Party had crafted a platform "that borrows quotations from the Bible and calls for faith in God," a platform "that bristles with moral turpitude."

Incredible to the point of being unbelievable, a New Jersey state representative complained at a budget hearing that spending on federal benefit programs was growing "at an excremental rate." And speaking of excremental rates, how about this news report?: "FECES RIGHTS. Appearing with Ronald Reagan at a New York anti-abortion gathering, Neil Bacon, chairman of N. D. Bacon Co., declared: 'Everybody who's for abortion was at one time themselves a feces. And that includes all of you out there. You were once a feces.'"

We all know a lovable relative, a bumbling sportscaster, or a dopey co-worker who mangles the language malappropriately. If these people were honest about the following tongue-tangles, they would say, "I resemble those remarks":

- A befuddled office manager trying to direct co-workers not to use the office photocopy machine without permission published this memorable memo: "Persons interested in using my secretary's reproductive equipment should contact me first."

- There was a slight drop in the number of marriage licenses applied for in Belmont County in 1976, compared to the previous year, but the number of marriages ending in divorce or disillusion subsided significantly.

- The cooking column is now being written by Karen Whatley, who replaces the late and lamentable Georgia Reardon.

- He really got my dandruff up.

- Bill Horner is arranging our annual speech contest. This year it'll be a bisexual affair.

- The committee compromised six dedicated people who really knew how to do their jobs.

- Careful, concise, sensitive, convicted, Martin is an able and committed pastor.

- He indicated his marriage was happy, as he and his wife have always been sexually combatible.

- He suffers from an insecuriority complex.

- It is obvious that women bear the grunt of the housework.

- Members of the Groveton Woman's Club gave the speaker a standing ovulation.

- The Mormons transgressed all across the U.S.

- My wife is a chronological liar.

- Sitting in a leather armchair in his office, Vogel considered the key attributes of a successful businessman. "Integrity, voracity, and spirituality," he almost snapped out.

- Mr. Nichols said the hunger problem began increasing during the last 12 to 14 months of the Carter presidency, but that the policies and programs of the Reagan administration exasperated that greatly.

- Ortiz is the Sailors' most recent recipient of the

pretentious Con Edison "Athlete of the Week" Award.

- Commenting on his occasional inconsistency, Red Sox pitching star Roger Clemens said, "When I get too much rest, I'm usually erotic."
- Evel Knievel will probably ejaculate while attempting to jump the Grand Canyon.
- I have a photogenic memory.
- The President of Dixville's Student Teacher Association has told the Legislative Education Committee a questionnaire distributed to Dixville's teachers showed that many used capital punishment in maintaining order in their classrooms.
- If you take this subject, you may be able to enroll in Harvard, Yale, or Prison.
- Economists said home builders and buyers remained skiddish about the real estate market.
- I am 5'7" when in full erection.
- They performed without musical accomplishment.
- If you broke the law five years ago, they cannot put you in jail anymore because of the statue of liberation.
- She sure has the wandering lust today.
- I was scared stiffless.
- College kids think they can use drugs with immunity.
- The girl was in the hospital having her utensils removed.
- A scout obeys all to whom obedience is due and respects all duly constipated authorities.
- Will my check be radioactive? Please verify.
- I figured you were home for the holidays when I saw that Vulva parked in the garage.
- You wouldn't want to live there. People conjugate at all hours.

- The loaf of bread had no adjectives and preservatives.
- The project was moving ahead rickety-split.
- A rainstorm reduced attendance at the parade and acted as a detergent to the crowds.
- Twenty-five years is a real millstone for anyone!
- For bulky letters we use vanilla envelopes.
- Sexual abuse can lead to more problems, one of which is insects.
- The club is used to hang out in, but problems do arise out of situations involving women. The first involves a written rule we have which states that no member shall, in any way, shape, or form, involve, or attempt to involve, himself with another member's girl. This rule has never been broken because it is explicitly stated and the wrongdoer knows that he will be dismembered for violating it.
- Graham College is dedicated to the principle of a balanced budget and cost containment. The creditability of its own internal financial management is regarded by Graham Administrators as imperative if the College is to be a leader in Business Management Education.
- My ancestors were pheasants who came over from France.
- On the day of his arrival, the pontiff is expected to celibate mass at Immaculate Conception Cathedral.
- I can't believe those guys on TV begging for money when they've got big houses, five or six cars, and Rolodex watches.
- The agents screamed anti-gay epitaphs throughout the attack.
- They've had quite a party here. Look at all the conundrums.

- I went to the doctor's office and he seduced my labor.
- Well, at least she's getting it out of her cistern.
- On you that coat just exhumes quality.
- Make your homecoming a memorial one.
- Here I was in the sanctimony of my own home.
- Now don't you be impotent to me!
- My wife gets very edgy when she's administrating.
- Students should practice safe sex by using condominiums.
- Their bodies were already noticeably thin and emancipated.
- There was an earthquake that measured seven on the ricochet scale.
- She is suffering from postmortem depression.
- When the temperature is below zero, it may feel even colder because of the windshield factor.
- I was able to recuperate my losses.
- In an emergency situation, call security at extension 3069, and we will determine if the situation is emergent.
- All meals include 8% tax and 17% gratitudes.
- The Japanese finally copulated to end World War II.
- He's an idealistic Don Coyote.
- I am boggled down with work.
- I think the condition is heretical; my grandfather had it.
- I discovered a new leash on life.
- It's all become a mute question.
- He leads a very sedimentary existence.
- I love academia nuts.
- The Galapagos Islands are regarded as the world's most famous living lavoratory.

- It's so important to avoid errors in grammar and usage that distract from your message.
- The king's robe was lined with vermin.
- After the homecoming queen is crowned, the band will strike up "Pomp and Circumcision."
- They thought she was 99 but are now convinced she is a centurion.
- In the film *When Harry Met Sally*, Harry and Sally have a Plutonic relationship.
- I am an expectant bride.
- Please tell me what to do about pimples. I have what is known as an inferiority complexion.
- We just got married on the spree of the moment.
- I am a young girl greatly desiring the company of the object sex.
- Some people are so dirty-minded that they purposely misconscrew every remark you make.
- Since 1985 Conti has taught Italian at the College of Grafton and in 1988 was benighted by the Italian government.
- I would urge the Director to seriously consider all that he says before he goes out in press, because so far all I've seen him do is make forepaws and ignoramus blunders!

Archie Bunker still shows up on our television sets in reruns, and the spirit of his garbled word-formation continues to suffuse our lives. Given the glut of forepaws and ignoramus blunders we English-speakers perpetrate and perpetuate, Archie's contributions to our language are absolutely memorial.

The Republic for Richard Stans

A teacher in elementary school read the following announcement to her class: "If you subscribe to the summer *Weekly Reader*, you will receive ten issues." One of her students waited all summer for a pair of tennis shoes.

A first-grade teacher had been sharing award-winning children's books with her class. Several days later one of her pupils said, "I have one of those books with the gold seals, you know, the winner of the cold cut award." What the child meant, of course, was the Caldecott Medal, awarded for most distinguished picture book for children.

A group of sixth-graders staged a shortened version of William Shakespeare's *Macbeth*. Out came the three witches cackling, "Double, double, toilet trouble!"

These incidents of verbal misapprehension remind me of my own misspelt youth, a time when one is likely to mishear popular sayings, proverbs, and song lyrics—"Miniza seen the glory of the coming of the Lord;/He has trampled out the vintage where the great giraffes are stored." Kids then start interpreting the boundaries that separate words in fresh, unconventional, and bizarre ways. As one student put

Our father, Art, in Heaven, Harold be thy name.

it, "If you can't write, how can you expect to get a pullet surprise?"

Like many other kids of my generation and any other, I inadvertently invented ingenious ways of making the sounds of words conform to my fantasy images, no matter what the words actually meant. I grew up saluting the flag each morning, along with millions of other schoolchildren who developed a warped view of America. Every school day I would pledge my unflagging allegiance to the republic for Richard Stans, joining generations of schoolchildren who made Richard Stans the most saluted man in the nation.

Many of my friends got to know the four witches. If you don't recognize them in the pledge you used to take, simply recall the line "to the republic four witches stand." Still others in our class pledged their legions to the flag, while the more imaginative among us led the pigeons to the flag.

Richard Stans must have a very strange republic because many of us back in public elementary school saluted one nation, underground, invisible while others offered their devotion to one naked individual.

Another name for the republic for Richard Stans was Tizovee, as in "My country, Tizovee . . ." In the Battle Hymn of that same Republic, my classmates and I sang lustily about the Lord tramping out the vintage with a great ceramic sword.

Those were the days when many of us strove to become valid Victorian of our class before going out into a doggy dog world. That was also the time when state law required that we recite the Lord's Prayer in public school. We knew God's first name was Art, or maybe Harold, because the prayer told us so: "Our father, Art, in Heaven, Harold be thy name." At each recitation we beseeched Art or Harold to keep us away from wicked New York City. How do I know? Because we asked him to "lead us not into Penn Station."

Some of us even asked Art or Harold to lead a snot into temptation.

Often our school assemblies featured a collective recitation of the Twenty-third Psalm, where we met a companion of Richard Stans, Art, and Harold. Her name was Shirley Murphy, and she appeared near the end of the psalm: "Shirley, good Mrs. Murphy, shall follow me all the days of my lives."

With piping voice, I used to sing a hymn about bringing in the sheeps and another called "Gladly, the Cross-Eyed Bear." Visions of a bear with a big smile (after all, his name was Gladly) and crossed eyes danced in my head. Only when I was older and could actually read the hymnal did I realize that the real words were "Gladly the Cross I'd Bear."

At Christmas I loved singing, "Good King Wences' car backed out on a piece of Stephen," "Chipmunks roasting on a open fire," "where shepherds washed their socks by night," and "Get dressed, ye married gentlemen, get huffing you this May."

During those holidays the Sunday school teacher asked us to draw a picture of the Nativity scene, I carefully sketched the figures of Mary, Joseph, and Jesus in the manger—and off to one side a fat guy. When the teacher asked who he was, I said, "Oh, that's Round John Virgin. He's the fellow who shows up in 'Silent Night'—'Round John Virgin, mother and child.' And he's got a buddy name of Vincent— 'Holy Vincent so tender and mild.'"

After that, I told the other kids in the class that I could name the ninth reindeer who pulled the sleigh of Santa Claus (also known as Sandy Claws).

"But there were only eight," chorused my classmates, "unless you count Rudolph."

"That's just it," I smugly announced. "Just listen to the song about Rudolph the Red-Nosed Reindeer, and you'll meet 'Olive, the other reindeer'!"

Here are some other misunderstandings of words and phrases by the young and not-so-young, dedicated to the memory of Richard Stans, Art, Harold be thy name, Shirley Murphy, a reindeer named Olive, and a cross-eyed bear called Gladly. Each mishearing is worthy of a pullet surprise. Each opens up a new world of meaning and imagination:

- With youth in Asia being a big question of right or wrong in today's society, hospitals fear that they will be sued.
- My grandfather suffers from Old Timer's Disease.
- He's cutting off his nose despite his face.
- She is laboring under a missed conception.
- If all the women sprayed their hair at the same time, how would it affect the O Zone?
- Eve's-dropping on the party telephone line was an accepted custom.
- The men were arrested for Mister Meeners.
- The dining room features the colors of seafoam green and mauve with Chip and Dale furniture placed throughout.
- They played Gershwin's *Rap City in Blue.*
- I came within a hare's breath of running for Congress.
- Proteins are composed of a mean old acid.
- They treated him as if he had the blue bonnet plague.
- Blacks are especially prone to suffer from sick as hell anemia.
- It was time to get up and Adam.
- In a pig's sty!
- It costs a nominal leg.
- Execution makes people escape coats of society.

- Michelangelo painted the ceiling of sixteen chapels.
- The Etruscans built a complex system of aquaducks.
- Ptolemy was the inventor of the sex tent.
- She's a real pre-Madonna.
- One of my favorite dishes as a child was cold slaw.
- He died of a harder tack.
- Green Bay's refreshing waters are at your beckoned call.
- WANTED: experienced GM Warranty Clerk. Including knowledge of micro fish.
- We can fix the leak with some duck tape.
- Matthews is an enthusiastic reader and claims "Lame is Rob," by Victor Hugo, as his favorite book.
- The woman wore a cow neck sweater.
- Spice up your omelet by adding some hollow penis.

Frequent fliers will undoubtedly sympathize with the passengers on a cross-country flight who were considering the announced luncheon choices of chicken Marengo, beef burritos, or fruit salad when the flight attendant added this useful piece of advice: "If you do not get your first choice, please do not be distressed, as all our entrees taste very much the same."

On another airline, customers were treated to this masterpiece of loopy logic: "If you are sitting in an exit row and you cannot read this card or cannot see well enough to follow these instructions, please tell a crew member"—in a flight safety booklet, in seven languages yet.

Life is not always logical—and neither is language. When people neglect to put their minds where their mouths are, the results vary from the amusing to the confusing. As one high-school student wrote, "I have to be aware of my mistakes so I can perfect them."

Vice President Dan Quayle, the man who gave the world "What a waste it is to lose one's mind, or not to have a mind is being very wasteful," generated a cult of Quayle-watchers ever on the lookout for symptoms of his foot-in-mouth disease:

It's not that I'm afraid to die. I just don't want to be there when it happens.—Woody Allen

- We are ready for every unforeseen event that may or may not occur.
- In the past we have tried too much to prevent the making of mistakes.
- We're going to have the best educated American people in the world.
- A word of advice: get a job.
- I'll tell you one person who doesn't think we've wasted our money on $600 toilet seats—Saddam Hussein.

Movie mogul Samuel Goldwyn was famous for memorable non sequiturs that somehow leapt over the chasm of illogic and landed on the side of insight:

- Spare no expense to make everything as economical as possible.
- Tell them to put more life into their dying.
- I don't care if my movie makes a cent. I just want every man, woman, and child in America to see it.
- Our comedies are not to be laughed at.
- I'm never going to write my autobiography as long as I live.

The tradition of running the mouth while switching off the brain continues unabated. Modern-day illogicalities are just as flighty as Quayle's and as good as Goldwyn's:

- "We have two incredibly credible witnesses here," announced Senator Joe Biden at the Clarence Thomas confirmation hearings. One of those unbelievably believable witnesses was now-Supreme Court justice Thomas, who repeatedly denied "*un*categorically" Anita Hill's allegations of sexual harassment.
- Argued law-and-order Philadelphia mayor Frank

Rizzo, who had also been chief of police, "The streets are safe in Philadelphia. It's only the people who make them unsafe."

- Jazz pianist and composer Eubie Blake smoked from the age of six and refused to drink water. On his hundredth birthday he observed, "If I had known I was going to live this long, I'd have taken better care of myself."

- On a National Public Radio interview, former attorney general Edwin Meese gave the world this mind-boggler: "One of the purposes of the primaries is for members of political parties to sort out their differences in areas in which they agree."

- Good pitching always stops good hitting, and vice versa.—Casey Stengel

- Thank God I am still an atheist.—Salvador Dali

- The only way we'll ever get a volunteer army is to draft 'em.—House Committee on Armed Services chairman F. Edward Hebert

- It belongs to us. We stole it fair and square.— Senator S. I. Hayakawa, who saw no reason to return the Panama Canal to Panama.

- Dear Ashamed in San Antonio: God cannot keep you from resisting temptation without your help. —Abigail Van Buren

- He's got a lot of depth on the outside, but deep down, he's shallow as hell.—another U.S. senator.

- We cannot fail to succeed.—Secretary of State James Baker

- It's not that I'm afraid to die. I just don't want to be there when it happens.—Woody Allen

- I love to see an audience panting breathlessly.— Johnny Carson

- I feel I did everything I could do, and probably more.—Atlanta Braves' manager Russ Nixon, shortly after being fired

- The problem of preserving chastity is as old as the human race.—from the introduction to *Sex Education and Training in Chastity* (1930)
- Fear was absolutely necessary. Without it, I would have been scared to death.—heavyweight champion Floyd Patterson, on the secret of his success.
- Of course, there must be subtleties. Just make sure you make them obvious.—Billy Wilder
- You won't find a single four-letter word in there. I don't go for that bullshit.—Hall of Fame pitcher Bob Feller, on his autobiography
- You won't hardly ever find a superachiever anywhere that wasn't motivated.—Ted Turner
- Experience shows that sweeping generalizations about broadcasting are invariably wrong.—London radio announcer
- We will be playing some pieces composed by Miles Davis prior to his death.—a Public Radio announcer
- I will defend anyone's right to agree with me.—Wisconsin state senator
- People in search of solitude are flocking here from the far corners of the world.—Canadian hotel prospectus
- The way my boy burns up tires, you'd think that rubber grows on trees.
- The Harvard doctors were not sure why saccharin makes rats sick but not humans, but they speculated the reason may simply be that rats are different from people.—Georgia news story
- Our office policy is that we will do our utmost to see patients in discomfort as soon as possible.—California dental newsletter
- If Martin Luther King were alive today, he'd be rolling over in his grave.
- The United States is the primary military power in the world. No one is second to us.

- If they ever take the emotion out of football, the stadiums will be full of no-shows.
- The instructions for the Illinois Motor Vehicle License Renewal begin, "CAUTION: You cannot take off the sticker after you put it on. Do not try to use glue to put it on." The very next statement informs the driver to "Remove as many of the old stickers from rear license plate as possible."
- I always wear my Guess jeans. In fact, I'd feel naked without them.
- One benefit of taking Latin is that you may come across someone who's been in a car crash, and they're trapped in the car, and all they can speak is Latin, and you couldn't help them because you couldn't understand them.
- Throughout the United States the differences between people are mainly the same.
- The driver of the car, Jennifer Thomas, was charged by police with drinking while intoxicated.
- Melissa P. Brophy, 48, and a parked car driven by Paul Stebbins were involved in an accident Saturday at 3:38 p.m.
- Nine times out of ten the official scorer will always call that a hit.
- Nothing new has changed.
- I will just die if nobody comes to my funeral.
- It was a case of too much moderation.
- She's been a born loser most of her life.
- Next time I send a fool to get something, I'll get it myself.
- Strategy is when you don't let the enemy know that you are out of ammunition, but keep on firing.
- Thanks to doctors, each generation is living longer than the one before it. Proof of this is the many more grandparents we see alive today as compared with great-grandparents.

- *Invisible Man* is a must-see.
- He said that 104 United States citizens visited his country between 1953 and 1954.
- This is the best film David Niven was in before he died.
- We're sending 23 million AIDS leaflets to every household in Britain.
- The topic for tonight's discussion is how to survive murder.
- If I had been instilled in the right principles of birth control, I would not now be the mother of an unwed baby.
- Being unique is a special quality found in everyone.
- Positive Air, a group of trampoline enthusiasts, will present an evening program emphasizing the importance of self-esteem, substance abuse, and achieving academic potential.—from an elementary school newsletter
- Foreman to mason: "Don't lay the bricks so close apart. Put them farther together."
- TO TOUCH THIS CABLE MEANS INSTANT DEATH   Violators will be prosecuted.
- TO OUR PATRONS   This week, the Saturday matinee will be held Tuesday instead of Thursday

Even famous writers goof. Daniel Defoe had his shipwrecked Robinson Crusoe (the only man who always got his work done by Friday) try to salvage some goods: "I resolved, if possible, to get to the ship; so I pulled off my clothes, for the weather was hot to extremity, and took to the water."

After the naked Crusoe climbs aboard ship, we read, "I found that all the ship's provisions were dry; and being well disposed to eat, I went to the bread room and filled my pockets with biscuits."

When Nobel Prize winner Eugene O'Neill wrote

his play *Where the Cross Is Made*, he gave these stage directions for one scene: "His right arm had been amputated at the shoulder and the sleeve on that side hangs flabbily. Then he goes over to the table, and sits down, resting his elbows, his chin in his hands, staring somberly before him."

Lest you think that life has gotten more logical, consider these news stories:

- In 1974, the Oxford City Library opened a new building, and they had it in operation for a few weeks before the official inauguration day. When Queen Elizabeth II finally showed up to do her job, a large notice at the library read CLOSED FOR OPENING.
- In 1984 a large section of the country was plunged into darkness by a blackout. Barbara Walters came on the CBS television news and announced, "If you are like most of the country, you do not have electricity."
- CBS is not the only network to broadcast tad-off-of-plumb statements that have a few screws loose and are missing some hinges. A 1988 NBC news item read, "The Supreme Court has been asked to review a request that prisons be allowed to use a lethal drug for injection for executions, even though the drug has not yet been approved as safe and effective for that purpose by the FDA."
- In 1991, an Illinois appeals court ruled that attorney Arthur Benjamin could not collect the entire amount he billed a female client for handling her divorce because some of the time he billed her for was for the two of them to have sex. Benjamin was also notified recently, by the Illinois Supreme Court, that he had been appointed to the Court's Committee on Character and Fitness.

❖ V ❖
Thud and Blunder

Mr. Potatoe Head

A Spell of Bad English

In January of 1992, President George Bush made a trip to Japan in an attempt to win concessions for United States trade. During a state dinner in Tokyo, Bush, smitten by a stomach flu, threw up on the pants of Japanese prime minister Kiichi Miyazawa. An article on the incident and the malady began, "When your insides are churning, the culprit is likely some virus or bacteria wrecking havoc in your intestinal tract."

Even though the president's intestinal passage was temporarily "wrecked" and the prime minister's pants now "reeked," the verb in the lead paragraph should have been spelled *wreaking*. Indeed, a misspelled word can wreak havoc on a written statement and wreck a reputation.

Five months after the incident, Vice President Dan Quayle came to a Trenton, New Jersey, elementary school to conduct a spelling bee. When a sixth-grader wrote *potato* on the blackboard, Quayle advised the boy to add an *e*.

Perhaps the spelling of Quayle's own last name confused him. Whatever the reason, commentators and comedians around the nation instantly began slicing him up by calling him "Mr. Potatoe Head."

Syndicated political cartoonist Jeff MacNelly de-
picted the orthographically challenged vice president wearing a "Quayl" button and pointing to a
blackboard with "Famly Valus" written on it.
Doonesbury cartoonist Garry Trudeau drew Quayle
rushing into a panel shouting, "Waite a minut!" *Tonight* host Jay Leno cracked, "Maybe the vice president should stop watching *Murphy Brown* and start
watching *Sesame Street*." Even the Brits went
Quayle-hunting when one English talk show host
claimed that the vice president's version of the children's ditty was "Old McDonald had a farm,
E-I-E-I-O . . . E."

At the Democratic nominating convention in New
York a month after the incident, a sign was displayed
that read, "Just Say Noe to Bush and Quayle." In his
acceptance speech at the end of the convention, Bill
Clinton poked fun at the spelling of his opponents
when he quipped, "He [George Bush] doesn't have
Al Gore, and I do. That's Gore, with an *e* at the end."
To his credit, the vice president struck back with humor and humility. During his own acceptance
speech at the Republican convention, he said of
Clinton and Gore, "If they're moderates, then I'm a
champion speller!"

Institutions can end up wearing a collective dunce
cap. During its 1990 graduation ceremonies, the
U.S. Naval Academy awarded diplomas to 990 mid-
shipmen and midshipwomen, but with a hitch
(which is just what one would expect from the
Navy). Each diploma read: "The Seal of the Navel
Academy is hereunto affixed."

The *Navel/Naval* spello became quite an embar-
rassment to an institution that is supposed to be running a tight ship in shipshape. Newsperson (or, in
this case, should we say anchorperson?) Diane Saw-
yer commented that the diplomas were apparently

written by people who didn't know their bell-bottoms from their belly buttons.

Orthographic pratfalls like these give new meaning to the warning that Phillip, fourth earl of Chesterfield, wrote to his son: "One false spelling may fix a stigma upon a man for life." Fortunately, I am able to present a ledger of jolly good spellos without stigmatizing the perpetrators:

- I have been raising the question for some years, but it is like the tree that falls in the dessert: Nobody hears it.
- Ever since the collapse of the Soviet Union there has been a considerable decline in the value of the rubble.
- The third year was a charm for Canton's eighth-grader Kurt Beiner, as he won the Middle School's spelling bee after correctly spelling "desicrate."
- Take pride: don't lose site of why you teach.—a message from the state's "Teacher of the Year"
- The next-door neighbors have a carousal on their patio.
- Is your back tired? Are your mussels sore?
- Taking this course will raise our essay tee scores. Higher essay tee scores are always a good thing.
- The grass on Templeton's recently built playing fields is being destroyed by hundreds of geese eating the new grass and fowling the area with their droppings.
- For the past two years, I have volunteered as a candy stripper in our local hospital.
- According to Postmaster Gerry Geiger, two out of every three Mill Valley citizens choose to pick their male up at the Post office, which is the obvious cause of the congestion.
- New York has added a new demention to my life.

- When she moved north from Georgia, he suffered withdrawl symptoms.
- The sailor was admired by his piers.
- Then spread the corn ears on the floor of an attic room that is hot and dry. Come November, slough the rock-hard corn colonels from the cob with gloved hands, then grind the corn in a clean coffee mill.
- Lounge: No Miners Allowed. ID's Required.
- *In another restaurant:* Please buss your own table.
- *In an ad for a full-service printer:* "A committment to excellence."
- Family Physician. Hours: 10:30–12:20–3:30–4:45, Monday–Friday, 10:30–11:45 Saturday. Limited Amount of Patience.
- In revoking Myers' pilot's license, the FAA cited Myers for "careless and wreckless operation of an aircraft."
- When planting seeds directly into the ground, water the soil before sewing.
- Vice President Quayle praised the Sandinista leader after Ortega handed over the reigns of government.
- She hadn't studied, so she prayed for a hurricane, a tornado, or a title wave, so she wouldn't have to take the test.
- Mrs. Rhodes becomes over rot when trying to manage her children.
- FOR SALE: Construction Wheel Barrel. $35.
- FOR SALE: ARABIAN MARE and two year old Philly, registered, pure bread.
- FOR SALE: 8-piece Ludwig drum set, includes symbols.
- FOR SALE: Green wing McCall and Minor Birds.
- Aunt and Roach Killer—$1.29.

- Our produce is low in fat—and good for your waste, too.
- *Sign on a New Hampshire grange hall:* No fighting or rowdiness aloud.
- This lasted until high school, where I found it necessary to get into a cliché in order to be accepted.
- Right now the team isn't sharp and I think we'll have to do some sole searching.
- Each nipple, embedded in the muscle, is connected by a short duck to the musk gland.
- I like looking at the colorful pieces of glass in my collide-o-scope.
- Jackie Kennedy grew up riding horses. She came from a well-manured family.
- *Posted at a school basketball court:* No black souls allowed.
- *On a Chinese fortune cookie:* You will gain admiration from your pears.
- He is recovering from a near-fatal accident that sent him into a comma.
- The boys in my class are just offal.
- Film—*Koenigsmark* (1935). A Ruritarian archduck is reported dead on a dangerous mission and his brother accedes to the throne.
- The issue of abortion does not belong in the government. We're back to arguing morals and morays that belong in church discussions.
- When I grow up, I want to be an architect who builds his own skycrapper.
- The board voted by telephone pole.
- I found a liter of pups.
- She lived in a small cabin and died a popper in 1935.
- Not responsible for tiepografical errors.

Does this spate of spellos augur a spellbound nation afflicted with increasing illiteracy? The following excerpts may offer an answer:

- Totally illeterate people cannot read or write their own names. Functionally illeterate people cannot read, write, or compute well enough to perform the common tasks of daily living. Illeteracy continues from one generation to another and is caused by a variety of educational, economic, and social reasons. Carlton has a greater percentage of illeteracy compared with that of the State of Maine's.
- In midevil times most people were alliterate.
- The people are now more liturate than the colonial days.
- Literarcy Week Observed.
- Help Irradicate Illiteracy.
- In addition to PUSH, the sisters of Alpha Beta Delta participated in four other philanthropic competitions. The first was a Bowel-A-Thon sponsored by the Gamma Epsilon Tau sorority for literacy.

How many times have you read a claim like "Prepare taste-tempting soups and salad that will wet the appetite and start any meal off on the right foot"? In advertisements like this one, the food is metaphorically compared to a whetstone that sharpens the knife's edge of the appetite, and the verb should be *whet*, meaning "to hone." Whenever I see *whet* misspelled as *wet*, I want to shout, "Great expectorations!"

Slips That Pass in the Type

Upset by all those typos you find in newspapers, magazines, and even books? Remember that even the most meticulous of printers has been plagued by gremlins since typesetting was first invented. In fact, the warning to "mind your p's and q's" comes into our language from the printing business. Apprentice typesetters were instructed to be careful in picking out letters that were often stored upside down. Under the pressure of deadlines, the *p* and *q* printer's blocks could easily be confused—and a word would come out puite botched uq.

Back in 1632, the gremlins slithered into a handsome edition of the Bible. Unfortunately, the little word *not* was omitted from the Seventh Commandment, making it read, "Thou shalt commit adultery." The luckless printers of this edition, which became famous as the Adulterous Bible, were fined 300 pounds, effectively putting them out of business. In 1716, thousands of copies of another Bible were published before it was discovered that the command to John, "sin no more," had been printed as "sin on more," a letter reversal with considerable appeal to sinners.

Even the great Bard of Avon's works haven't been

FOR SALE: 8,500-pound power wench and a queen-size water bed.

exempt from reversals of fortune—and reversals of letters. The fourth folio edition of _Hamlet_, published in 1685, has a beaut right on the title page, in display type measuring about twenty points high:

THE
TRAGEDY
OF
HAMLET
RPINCE OF DENMARK

Lest you think that a more literate population aided by computer spell-checkers has banished the typo gremlins from today's publications, have a look at some modern-day typos. You'll find that the resluts are the same:

- Although a conventional cast-iron sink is available for around $200, you will pay more for larger sizes, multiple bowels, vibrant colors, or special materials.
- An in-debt discussion of the new tax laws is available by using the order blank in the tax return package or by calling 1-800-424-3676.
- Gordie Jefferson celebrated his birthday last week with a party for eight little fiends.
- Following are the types of commercial enterprises that are banned: 1. Any type that pollutes by affluent or smoke.
- A catafalque is a coffin draped in black crap.
- The best treatment for shock is to rape the patients in blankets.
- He received his graduate degree in unclear physics.
- And during the current fiscal year, Kinney plans to increase the number of uninformed sergeants by 14, making a total of 42.

- The commander had a firm but genital hold on his men.
- At that point the gallery of golf fans deserted the championship to watch Miss Farley, whose shorts were dropping on the green with remarkable regularity.
- The conference's attitude was indicated by the almost total lack of applause after Mr. Wilson's 30-minute speech while Engineering Union leader Bryan Stanley was greeted with sustained crapping when he put the anti-common market case.
- Catholic nuns of the Mission of Jesus, Mary, and Joseph, with a television success behind them and Mother Superior Carlotta at the guitar, are bidding here for fame and fortune in the pope charts.
- The deceased retired in 1982 from United Airlines where he was the foreman in the turban shop.
- What Mrs. Thatcher's closest friends are wondering is whether, as the signs suggest, she is suffering from metal fatigue.
- Enjoy our breath-taking view of the Atlantic Ocean that is eliminated by our special lighting at night.
- Playboy Enterprises estimates that removing ornamental pants from its offices will save $27,000 a year.
- It is said that there are more golf curses per square mile in North Carolina than anywhere else in the world.
- Busy lawyer seeks alert young woman to serve as deceptionist.
- Successful widower, aged 44, usual trappings, nonsmoker with varied interests, seeks affectionate female to shave the enjoyable things in life.

- Feeling tired and lustless?
- Hot males delivered to your home in minutes.
- The welcoming reception for all delegates will begin at 8 p.m. Hors d'oeuvres and drinks will be served. Souses are welcome.
- Mrs. Floyd Garneau died yesterday at the age of 69. She was a well known fan of the Boston Red Sox, for whom she rotted for years.
- Ruby Nell, the 200 lb. wild hog who loves moon pies and Pepsi-Cola, is also fond of candy canes off a Christmas tree. Here Ruby Nell gets an early holiday teat from her owner Vicki.
- She says she wants this store and all others selling pornography barred because such material is contrary to Judo-Christian values.
- Alexander's screen career began with her portrayal of James Earl Jones' wife in "The Great White Hop."
- Found: One white rabbi with brown ears. Found hopping down 3rd Avenue.
- In front of a Dearborn, Michigan, church: "Millions long for immorality and don't know what to do on a rainy day."
- Throughout the day there will be hands-on craft sexhibits and entertainment at various locations around the State House.
- Happy Valley Kennel Club held their September meeting at Scuffey's Restaurant in Plattsburg. Several members exhibited their dongs at the Stanley Kennel Club A Match.
- A bottle of whiskey and a bottle of sherry, together worth $25 were stolen by a gurglar who forced open a window of a house on Greenfield Avenue last night.
- To acquaint employees with Markham Tire's group of general foremen, we will try to report

the personal histories of these important clogs in our plant machinery.

- Would She Climb to Top of Mr. Everest Again? Absolutely!
- District Attorney Vernon Batchelder will address the women's prison council at noon, Thursday. He will speak on "Women and the Criminal Lay."
- Fed Up With High Heating Bills? Will McBain Complete Hating Specialists.
- FOR SALE: 8,500-pound power wench and a queen-size water bed.
- Jason Thompson, who had four RBIs in August, four in September and one homer since July 26, smashed a blast off a poet high in the upper deck for his grand slam.
- Senator George McGovern of South Dakota, also campaigning for the primary, appealed for the votes of blue-colored workers in Milwaukee.
- I'm developing muscles under the armpits from the constant use of crotches.
- Alexander Hamilton was George Washington's closet companion.
- David Cone's one-hitter was all but overshadowed by his rookie teammate'shitting.
- He is a charismatic speaker and a major farce in politics.
- Texatron is to get $1,500,000 via the Northern Ireland Office to keep the textiles and carpet yarn factory open for another seven moths.
- Many parties and showers honor Marianne Lawton and finance Kent Sorokin.
- CREATIVE DOUGH—Learn the art of using yeast dough to create rounded, crusty, fragrant French loves and rolls.
- The award, $5,000 and a plague, is presented each year to a scientist or engineer for scientific

achievement and for contributions to the advancement of knowledge.

- Not that anyone accused Maston himself of being a racist. It was just that political timidity, or some inexplicable force, pushed him into the Dixiecrap camp whenever a crucial vote arose that involved racial and regional passions.
- Debris from the collapse of the Harbor Freeway bride caused a huge traffic jam about 10 miles south of downtown Los Angeles.
- From September 17. The Fabulous New Production of OKLAHOMO!
- Mrs. Clarence Greenough looked particularly neat and smart in her A.W.V.S. uniform after a long lay at headquarters.
- ON THIS DATE: IN 1870 Ada H. Kepley of Effingham, Ill., became America's first female.
- Take Highway 1 to Paloma exit. Then go right on Palmetto Blvd. and, viola!, there you are.
- EXTERMINATING: We are trained to kill all pets.
- Porpoises converse in complicated patterns of whistles, clivkd, sdsvsn mimiu dpokra Isnhushrd.

No typo could be more terrible, of course, than the one in a telegram that a man away on a business trip sent to his wife: "Having a wonderful time. Wish you were her."

FOR SALE: Very unique home in downtown Craigsville. Large lot. Many trees. One you will enjoy living in.

Grammar Stammers

At a recent meeting of the American Association for the Advancement of Science, researchers unveiled their finding that a single dominant gene controls the ability to learn the rules of grammar. These days, it seems, more and more people, even in high places, are getting caught with their genes down and their loose sentence structure exposed:

The principal of a Long Island school sent thousands of flyers to parents inviting them to a meeting titled "Everything You Wanted to Know About High School But Was Afraid to Ask."

A Fort Wayne anchorperson announced, "The Hoosier State, like many other states across the nation, are not making the grade when it comes to education."

The *New Orleans Times-Picayune* reported, "Statewide, students performed extremely poor on the writing section of the exam."

In cases like these, we say, "No wonder!,"—and we scratch our heads at the grammar stammers so prominently displayed in our nation's newspapers and magazines:

- During the summer, my sister and I milked the cows, but now that school has started, my father milks the cows in the morning, and us at night.

- Mrs. McAllister watched as the giant airplane taxied out of the gate. Then like some wild beast she pointed her nose down the runway and screamed terrifically into the sky.

- Mr. Yoshiko said the donkey owners should clearly state why they want to keep the animals. "If they cannot give good reasons why they need the donkeys, then they will be shot."

- *From a John Simon film review of* The Last of the Mohicans: The film was shot in North Carolina's Blue Ridge Mountains, as photogenic as Dolly Parton's knockers, and Dante Spinotti's camera has caught them, now enveloped in teasingly veiled morning mists, now bursting forth in sun-kissed orange voluptuousness.

- *From an ad for a community health center:* How to talk to your kids about sex, even if you've never done it before.

- Dr. Wallace suggests it is up to GPs to broach sex with teenagers. "I now routinely ask teenagers whether they have ever had sex as part of the consultation, and I usually get a good response."

- DEAR DR. KASMIROV: I'm 18 years old and have had sex for the first time. Although it lasted only about three minutes, is it possible I could get pregnant?
  DEAR READER: Yes. Have a pregnancy test done by your doctor or a clinic, or test yourself by using one of the home kits sold in most drug stores. If the result is negative, do it again in a week or so.

- It is my hope in the near future to show additional films on the hazards of cigarette smoking, nutrition, and dental care.

- Princess Anne is the daughter of Queen Elizabeth II and a noted equestrian performer.

- We have turned cans into cash to use towards programs for our children, rather than burying them in a landfill. Aluminum cans have generated $65,359.00 since the spring of 1989 for our school.

- There is a real need for a Woman's Health Clinic on campus. This clinic would provide help for those with V.D. and those who want some form of birth control. It will not increase promiscuity but rather help those who really need it.

- Place garbage in this barrel. It will be here weekends for your use.

- FOR SALE: Very unique home in downtown Craigsville. Large lot. Many trees. One you will enjoy living in.

- Recent visitors were the Jonathan Goldings and their in-laws the Brett Packards, from Lake Placid, NY. Brett had his tonsils removed in Centerville. It was a pleasant surprise to have them for supper.

- *Last line of a short story by a famous author:* "On the floor above him lived a redheaded instructor in physical education, whose muscular calves he admired when they nodded to each other, by the mailbox."

- DEAR HELOISE: Every time I see a dog riding unrestrained in an automobile or the back of a pickup truck, it infuriates me. I wonder how many of them would let their children travel like that!

- Officials attend Port Charlotte's Betty Barnstead after breaking her arm in yesterday's judo competition.

- It is estimated that one out of every 100 women between the ages of 12 and 25 are anorectic, one

out of seven are bulimic, and between 5 and 10%
are male.

- I haven't liked the food in any of the cafeterias
  I've eaten.
- A funeral ceremony can accumulate significant
  costs such as cleaning the church and an organist.
- In what may be a precedent-setting case in Wisconsin, a Madison woman is seeking $500,000
  from the man who raped her and his mother's
  homeowner's insurance company.
- To stop rumors about his questionable sexual
  proclivities, he [Oscar Wilde] married and then
  fathered two sons in rapid succession.
- Flames destroyed a small barn used as a garage,
  a vehicle and sporting equipment at the Robert
  Strauss residence off Goodrich Road here Sunday.
- A want ad in a Maine Swap and Sell Guide
  grimly illustrates the macabre results of a missing apostrophe: "WANTED: Guitar for college
  student to learn to play, classical non-electric,
  also piano to replace daughters lost in fire."

Don't Dangle Your Participle
in Public

In the film version of *Mary Poppins*, Bert the Chimney Sweep tells Uncle Albert, "I know a man with a wooden leg named Smith."

"What's the name of the other leg?" Albert asks with a laugh, and the misplaced phrase "with a wooden leg named Smith" becomes a running joke through the movie.

Following the 1992 Los Angeles riots, this photo caption appeared: "President Bush gestures while telling an anecdote about violent crime at a Republican fund-raiser in Philadelphia."

Where did the violent crime happen? In the streets, of course, and not at the Republican fund-raiser. Such sentences are afflicted with misplaced modifiers, meaning that their scaffolding is firmly planted on midair.

In a major New England newspaper appeared this cryptic listing: "Former hostage Terry Waite talks about five years of confinement in Beirut with Barbara Walters in a specially expanded segment of *20/20* at 10 on Channel 5." Misplaced modifiers seem to be especially attracted to Ms. Walters. In *Anguished English* the prominent news journalist appeared in this sentence: "Yoko Ono will talk about

We saw many bears driving through Yellowstone Park.

her husband, John Lennon, who was killed in an interview with Barbara Walters."

Just before takeoff, a flight attendant announced over the public address system: "I have a pearl earring from a passenger I found on the floor." Presumably, it was the earring—and not the passenger—that the tangle-tongued flight attendant had found on the floor. Here are some more mangled modifiers found on the floor, in the closet, and in a number of other strange places:

- *From a news story about former heavyweight champion Mike Tyson:* According to Anderson, Williams is Tyson's friend and should have known of Tyson's history as a serial buttocks fondler of black women, and a perpetrator of lewd and disrespectful acts against black women of the most vulgar type.
- Although irregular, we will consider your request.
- Oxbridge Church tries to assist in serving a luncheon for the families of church members who have died immediately following the funeral.
- Following the brawl at 5 East Broad St., Detective Delvecchio said, Officer Michael Murphy of the Farmington Police drove down Orchard Street with his department's police dog addressing the crowd.
- A woman who started selling hot dogs clad in a bikini two weeks ago was denied a vendor's license at a Town Council meeting.
- Another surgeon performed an amputation of the leg with the patient hypnotized four years later.
- After investigating, Greenfield found that the Volkswagen was registered to Schmidt's girlfriend that he had been using.
- The couple gets their antiques from a buyer in

Los Gatos who accepts antiques on consignment from local persons in good condition.

- You can own a handcrafted etching in glass for a limited time only.
- A giant painting of a Mexican couple astride an unhappy horse which was salvaged from the old Santa Barbara Biltmore hotel hangs prominently on one wall.
- The new facilities will make it possible for babies to be born in Roosevelt Hospital for the first time.
- She watched as her father returned home with the horses all dressed in cowboy attire.
- Photo caption: Seen from a vaporetto: a gondola with a liveried gondolier carrying a middle-aged woman and an elderly man.
- During our entire marriage of 44 years, plus a few preceding years of courtship, I could count the number of times Henry was stopped by a policeman for driving on just three fingers of my left hand.
- A convicted sex abuser was sentenced to life in prison with the possibility of parole on Monday.
- Philip Margoles, 61, died Monday after a long illness at a local hospital, where he had been a patient for four days.
- It is time to renew the Denver city license for your pet, which expires in a month.
- A federal court jury Tuesday rejected a $10 million lawsuit filed against the Nissan Motor Corporation by relatives of a woman who claimed she was decapitated by her Sentra's automatic shoulder harness.
- Please take time to look over the brochure that is enclosed with your family.
- An oil spill was first reported to the Coast Guard in early May by a person who saw oil covered rocks walking along the shore.

- The Pleasant Lane School opened Sept. 6 to house fourth- and fifth-graders after being moth-balled for five years.

- The Sterling Recreation Department will begin selling tickets to see the Red Sox play at 6:30 p.m. in the Town Hall.

- An owner of a Greenwich Village barbershop survived being shot in the neck as he slept by a gunman who broke into his house at Queens.

- The bride was given in marriage by her father, wearing a Victorian style dress with cathedral length train.

- A man who videotaped a couple having sex through partially open blinds can get the tape back in 20 days, a judge ruled.

- *Midnight Express* is a movie about a man who escaped from a Turkish prison where he had been mistreated with the help of his girlfriend.

- Wednesday morning, Gordon's oldest son Bill signed a national letter of intent with Indiana University to play football for the Hoosiers in the family kitchen at 1374 Pond Drive in West Carston.

- An investigation of the shooting, in which Vincent was killed, by 30 members of the Portland Police Department, showed the following. . . .

- Since opening about six months ago, I've eaten with my wife at the Thu Hong Restaurant ten times and have always enjoyed the food.

- During the height of the annual summer spawning runs, Ronnie Ackerman photographed a brown bear wallowing for salmon in a secluded Alaskan stream with a Nikkormat camera and 300mm lens.

- Through the use of ultrasound, University of Washington researcher Marcia Greene studies women who develop high blood pressure during pregnancy with the assistance of ALAA-Washington funds.

- He ran outside and chased after the cat with a broomstick in his underwear.
- Oh, still, it was delicious to sit near the well where a few trees had struggled and survived, gnawing on the salty stringy meat and drinking beer.
- Grilled in foil or alongside a ham, turkey, or chicken, those who shied away from onions before will delight in this newfound vegetable.
- The Bush administration proposed the most drastic overhaul of banking laws since the Great Depression yesterday.
- Hunters have gained the right to hunt deer in the Illinois Supreme Court.
- At 5:20 yesterday evening, Sean Leary, 24, of Belmont Road, was driving his motorcycle west on the street where he lives at a high speed.
- St. Pierre confirmed that the commission has hired a private investigator to check allegations about Jacobs, who was suspended for 45 days with pay on Halloween.
- Hidden in the dining room breakfront, in a blue-enameled box bedecked with hand-painted flowers, Miriam Dagle keeps the keys to 18 neighbors' houses.
- The Tennessee Bureau of Investigation presented an eight-inch thick report on the alleged involvement of Vanderbilt University officials in the distribution of illegal anabolic steroids to District Attorney Paul Rizzo.
- A decade after his untimely death, a goal which he worked hard to establish, the awarding of an annual scholarship to individuals pursuing real estate as a profession, has come to its fruition.
- In June 1989, barely capable of uttering an En-

glish phrase, Martinez's hand was severed at the wrist in a construction accident.

- Johnson would press for repeal of the unenforceable, circa-1848 laws on the books that prescribe criminal penalties against women who have abortions along with their physicians.

- Mrs. Gruber was one of eight children born to F. R. and Gretchen Kremen on September 20, 1993, in Kingston.

- Sayer's frozen sculptures double as serving vessels. They are preserved in a cavernous freezer, and come Saturday evening, they are rolled out into a room-full of people, laden with iced shrimps and fresh fruits.

- Dear Abby: I was so depressed that I considered suicide on a daily basis.

- A new security device can detect a person approaching your home right through the walls.

- We saw many bears driving through Yellowstone Park.

A Guide for Blooper Snoopers

Medieval physicians believed that the state of one's health was determined by a balance of mysterious fluids called "humors." Today there is considerable evidence that humor, in the modern sense, is indeed a tonic for health. Among that evidence are the mailbags of letters I've received from hospitals, hospices, and rehabilitation wards around the world describing the use of *Anguished English* for the healing power of its laughter.

That is why I have written *More Anguished English* and why I hope someday to write a sequel to this sequel. As humor guru Joel Goodman has pointed out, "Seven days without laughter makes one weak."

Because each blooper in the *Anguished English* series is real, I rely on the kindness of strangers to send me the raw material for these books. If you would like to contribute to *Even More Anguished English*, please mail your best bloopers to:

Richard Lederer
5 Merrimack St.
Concord, NH 03301

As with any form of humor, one can find goofs that cause readers to self-detonate with uncontrollable laughter and gaffes that have all the impact of a Styrofoam pebble falling onto a pond. Some examples are delightfully wiggy and completely believable. Others are awkward and of doubtful authenticity.

I have appointed myself sole judge of blooperistic perfection. To help all you super-duper blooper snoopers to select which goodies to send me, I offer a concise guide and official grading system. No item winged my way is ever stigmatized with a failing grade, but only solid A's and B's make it into the pages of *Anguished English* books.

The nonblooper:

- "The criteria is the person who most believes in his or her own publicity." The plural form of *criteria* creates a usage error, but the faulty word choice is not a blooper. Bloopers require the co-existence of two meanings—one intended and one unwitting—that are both held in the reader's mind. No such double entendre exists here. Grade: D–.
- "We are all human, but our ideas are different." A wise observation, but where are the multiple meanings and the humor? Whatever this submission is, it isn't a blooper. Grade: D.

The unfunny blooper:

- "My boyfriend gave me a quart watch for Christmas." The confusion between *quart* and *quartz* legally qualifies this statement as a blooper, but so what? Grade: C–.
- "I enjoy watching the stars and pointing out the consolations." The inadvertent substitution of

consolations for *constellations* is a tad more wiggy than the *quart-quartz* mix-up, but once again the example simply isn't funny. Grade: C.

The genuinely funny blooper:

• "The first World War was caused by the assignation of the Arch-Duck by an anahist." Now the battery of verbal faux pas—*assignation, Arch-Duck* and *anahist*—starts the laugh motor. Grade: B.

• "The mountain is named for the Rev. Starr King, who was an invertebrate climber and author of the book *The White Hills*." This is not only the most spineless blooper I've ever encountered; it's also a real knee-slapper. Grade: B+.

The fall-on-your-butt-with-laughter blooper:

• "This being Easter Sunday, we will ask Mrs. White to come forward and lay an egg on the altar." Here the expression "lay an egg" zaps us simultaneously at the levels of the literal and the fowl. The harmony of both witty and unwitting humor creates a delightful pullet surprise. Grade: A.

• "Sir Francis Drake circumcised the world with a 100-foot clipper." The two inadvertent puns are hilarious, sexy, and thoroughly believable. How blunderful it is that one student's innocent incompetence can produce such nautical naughtiness. This sentence is one of the greatest bloopers ever blooped. Grade: A+.

About the Author

Richard Lederer has published more than a thousand articles and books about language, including his best-selling *Anguished English* and *Get Thee to a Punnery*.

"The World According to Student Bloopers," a chapter in *Anguished English*, has been the most folk-Xeroxed and E-mailed piece of humor in the United States. *Get Thee to a Punnery* earned Dr. Lederer election as International Punster of the year for 1989–90. He was voted joke-telling champion of New York in 1991 and was runner-up in the national competition in 1992.

His weekly column, "Looking at Language," appears in newspapers and magazines throughout the United States. He is the Grammar Grappler for *Writer's Digest*, associate editor of *The Farmer's Almanac*, and language commentator on National Public Radio. He has been profiled in publications as diverse as *The New Yorker*, *People*, and *The National Enquirer*.